SKINS

Oxblood, Sweat and Beers

IAN PHILLIPS

NEW HAVEN PUBLISHING LTD UK

First Edition
Published 2016
NEW HAVEN PUBLISHING LTD
www.newhavenpublishingltd.com
newhavenpublishing@gmail.com

The rights of Ian Phillips, as the author of this work, have been asserted in accordance with the Copyrights, Designs and Patents Act 1988.

Cover design © Pete Cunliffe
pcunliffe@blueyonder.co.uk

newhaven
publishing

Contents

Skins Oxblood, Sweat and Beers

FOREWORD

 The first time I saw a skinhead (or I should say skinheads) was as a young impressionable 8 year old way back in 1970. I was making my way to Finsbury Park with some friends for a pre-arranged afternoon of '3 & in' when I saw two long haired youths (maybe they were grebos?) being chased along the Seven Sisters Road by about five or six skins looking to engage with them in a little 'Bovver ' or 'aggro'! I can remember it like it was yesterday, when in fact it was 45 years ago but the plain truth is it began a lifetime's love and fascination with the cult they call...SKINHEAD.

I have spent the last four decades making Ska and Reggae music, working with skinhead idols like Prince Buster, Laurel Aitken and Judge Dread and the music that I have been making since 1986 as King Hammond is mostly aimed at the skinhead fraternity. In 1987 I wrote a song called "Skinhead Love Affair" which, nearly 30 years after it was conceived, still gets the skins on the dance floor.

When I think of a skinhead I think of someone who has style, loves their music and walks through life with a swagger.

---Nick Welsh
Songwriter & Producer

FOREWORD

 Its 1969 and I had just come back from gigging up North. I felt an urgency to write songs, not just songs, but songs aimed at my new found fans - the Skinheads. Those following days and weeks changed the whole outlook of The Pyramids. We were a very successful band, having hit the British charts with 'Train Tour to Rainbow City'. Seeing a significant change at our shows, these strange kids with braces and boots brought fun to our gigs. It was love at first sight and so I got around the piano and started composing 'Skinhead Girl', 'Must Catch a Train', 'Stay with Him', Skin Flint', and arranged 'These Boots Were Made for Stomping' and the anthem of the Skins: 'SKINHEAD MOONSTOMP'.

I wanted to be a part of this culture, a group of kids who embraced my Jamaican Music. And I say until this day, Skinheads kept Jamaican music alive and kicking (no pun intended). We had a saying which was adopted by the great Laurel Aitken, that if we see one Skinhead in the audience then we felt good because we knew it's gonna be one hell of a night. I must say we all felt this urgency and love for our new friends and fans. The whole band – Frank, Mick, Josh, Roy – and even our Road Manager to this day are stuck in the culture and basking in it. My song *SPIRIT OF 69* encompasses that period and is still an influence...yes 1969.

--Monty Neysmith
Songwriter & Producer

FOREWORD

 I was a young teenager when my dad first said 'Hey, Boy, you're too rude'. This was his way of telling me I was too rebellious for his liking and his strict ways, at home. I left home at fifteen but took much of my dad's style with me. This was the very Jamaican sharp suits, trilby or pork-pie hat and good shoes. It was like you always looked ready for a special event, even if you were just hanging out with mates; and more importantly, even if you were flat out broke, looking expensive was what we all did, regardless.

The whole Rude Boy has two meanings to it. Being rude was just as it sounds. You didn't want to conform, you rebelled and you got into all kinds of trouble. The other meaning was more about the clothes, the music scene and the swagger. I was probably part of both meanings, although veered more to the fashion and music once I got out of borstal and fighting scene.

I can see why many became skinheads because of The Specials. Our lyrics and tough style tuned into the youths of that time. We had a social and political message, something you don't really get these days, even though we are now in similar times to the Thatcher Britain we were in then.

We had some great skinheads and rude boys and girls into the music who have followed me for years. They knew we were about being rude, being united and being socially aware of the equal fight we were all going through at that time. Remember, some of these guys or their parents had also followed the late 60s early reggae vibes long before The Specials. I grew up on the stuff they were listening to and played my Jah Baddis sound system to all kinds of crowds, before The Specials too. The Jamaican music was evident around all great dances, whether a Caribbean style event or a Skinhead dance. The Specials created even more unity through music, I guess.

In every walk of life there will always be the trouble-makers. This was no exception at The Specials' gigs. The racist type of skinhead probably nicked the look, because, let's face it, it's a tough look and great for appearing tougher and more aggressive. These guys would enjoy the music and even sing along, then halfway through start trouble and stir up racial tension. Now remember, they have come to a gig to watch and hear a mixed band of black and white fellas, doing great things with reggae, ska and punk, to later act like they hated us for what we stood for. That's after a night of dancing and singing along. Most were just boneheads with no real sense; others were just following mates or later realised it was all shit and hypocritical, so moved over more to the original skinheads' stance, like the rude boys and girls.

On many occasions I confronted the boneheads, often after diving off the stage into the crowd for a good punch up. I actually used to enjoy an excuse to beat the fuck out of some dickhead. It got a bit out of hand at a few gigs, though, but I refused to let the few spoil it for the masses.

I remember a big fight which was nicknamed the 'Primrose Hill Massacre' in Coventry. This was just before we got The Specials thing going. Some of the local black guys were getting trouble every time they went out by certain gangs of racist-type skinheads. If you were on your own, you got it even worse. I remember being on my own one time and grabbing one of the three skins who started on me on the Hollyhead Road, by the throat in a special grip, and walking him all the way to the door of our youth club, where my mates were. I told the other two to back off or I would choke their friend. I let him go once I was with my friends, so making it a more equal fight. Anyway, those attacks became more and more frequent, so my friend Trevor, brother Franklyn, and other mates all planned an ambush. We set it up so that about eight of the skins chased one of the guys into

Primrose Hill, where we were all hiding. What followed was a massive and very bloody fight. Most of us got arrested and sentenced for all kinds of affray and assault charges.

The funny thing is, many years on, we still see those guys and even get invited to events and reunions. Many of them got hurt quite badly, but they say it's all in the past and it was just one of those things. Fighting for freedom to walk the street without fear of attack and standing your ground. That's all it was really.

I know for a fact that the skinhead scene as a whole is not a racist scene and it's a shame that it often gets tarred like that. I have friends and family who have been skinheads for years and have embraced the sounds of Jamaican music, as well as embraced me as a solo artist and my music with The Specials. Even my wife, Christine Sugary, although mixed race, was a skinhead in her teens when I was her pin-up. She later called herself a Rude Girl, even though she had a shaven head and wore all the clothing. She was based in London then and would go to clubs and parties where skinheads (black and white) would dance together, share records, and enjoy the scene, with black and white friends. We both still have so many skinhead friends and fans who enjoy the rudy/skinhead cross-over of fashion, style and music. With the Jamaican influence to the original skinhead style and culture, how could it ever be considered racist? Only a bonehead would think like that, or the press who stir up divisions. I guess things won't change unless the skinheads who don't agree with or like to be around racism take a stand.

Neville Staple, The Specials

FOREWORD

I grew up in in a coal mining village just outside of Coventry so I was aware of Skinheads from the early days, as most of the youngsters there were Skinheads. Me and my friends lived in the council house road and we all had long hair in the late 1960s/early 1970s. With The Specials supporting the Clash and Sham 69, we noticed the right-wing National Front was recruiting Skinheads and Jerry Dammers thought we should be an alternative. Jerry had already got Horace Panter to adopt the Skinhead look by the time I joined the group in 1978. Horace was hardly working class, but he looked the part just as long as nobody heard his middle class accent, lol. I was a punk rocker in those days, but after the Clash tour we all adopted the Rude Boy/Mod-Skinhead look.

With the Skinhead scene it was always hard to know from a distance the good Skinheads from the bad right-wing Skins. We had many friends/fans that were nice left-wing Rude Boys but sometimes we would encounter the other sort. A lot has been made about this over the years and yes, there was trouble at some shows but it wasn't always with the right-wing elements. Sometimes it was just plain old football violence: gangs of lads from different parts of the country would start chanting their team name and it would all kick off.

Today I play all over the UK, Europe and the States and I'm glad to say it's been a long time since I met any bad Skins. In fact, some of my best friends are Skinheads. I guess it must look funny when people see a Rockabilly chatting and having a few beers with Skinheads, but we have more in common than not nowadays.

--Roddy Byers, The Specials

10

Introduction

Skinhead! -- What does it stand for? Racism? Patriotism? Often racism and patriotism can both get confused with one another. Or is it more solidarity, unity and a reflection of working class pride? The answer to all these questions is not an easy one. It has been written before that every subculture is a mass of contradictions, and the skinhead culture is certainly no exception. Books have been written, films have been made, and endless stories painting a rather ugly picture of the culture as a whole have been endlessly spewed out by the media. The word Skinhead often provokes an intense feeling of fear and hatred for many, but why? In writing this book, I wanted to present a clear, better-rounded view of the British skinhead scene from the past to the present. While it's far from a fairy tale, as the scene is hardly made up by choir boys and girls, I wanted to present that there is inevitably good and bad everywhere, unfortunately. If a white man was to savagely attack a black man over the colour of his skin, does that necessarily make all white people racist?

After having conducted a series of interviews and drawn stories from many skinheads – both coming from its original inception in the late 1960s through to present-day skinheads – there is one constant running theme throughout their tales of life as a skinhead. For many, it's a way of life, the allure of belonging to something, brotherhood, a genuine love of the music and the fashion that has shaped the whole skinhead culture. No racism. The scene is multi-cultural. This is at the heart of skinheads. Yet there have been some stories that contradict this: the allure of being in a gang made those who were part of it feel as though they had power and a voice. Football violence, for instance, had been prevalent, but not by all skinheads, of course. And football hooliganism certainly can't be blamed squarely on skinheads, as many that had – or have-no connections to the scene love inciting violence and riots on an opposing team of football

11

supporters. A so-called sport some skinheads loved to indulge in in the early days was "Paki-bashing" and "queer-bashing". Yet, once again, while there are no excuses to be made for these acts of violence, it can hardly be said that these are acts primarily undertaken by just skinheads.

For the real skinhead the scene is a positive thing and stems back to what I said earlier about a sense of belonging, an intense passion for the music and the fashion, having fun and showing loyalty to one another. The real skinhead will describe those that blackened the scene's name by racially-motivated attacks on Asian and black people as "bone heads". As the years went by, and in the Thatcher-run era in the 1980s, the skinheads communed together, the scene seen as an affront to a repressive political system, and a reflection of the working-class despair. However, there were the extremists that wanted to claim England as their own and staunch supporters of the National Front and BNP, often seen on protest rallies. These images became a fixation in the media and subsequently (and sadly) distorted many people's views of the skinhead scene. Propaganda reared its ugly head in magazines such as *People*, with a quote in a 1986 issue reading: 'Saturday night fear strikes scores of European cities – even behind the Iron Curtain – every week. It's the night when the packs of ultra-racist, ultra-fascist skinheads take to the streets, ready to kick, bash, knife and shoot kids, families and pensioners.'

Really? With words like that its little wonder that people (unfortunately) tarred all skinheads with the same brush. Is it true? Absolutely not. Yes, racism and fascism has infiltrated into the skinhead culture. But real skinheads will argue (quite rightly) that these vigilantes took the whole meaning of being a skinhead out of context. Yet if you were to do a general survey with the British public about what their thoughts are of the skinhead movement, several responses would be "racist thugs", "lager louts", "yobbos", "dole dossers". This is grossly unfair to the many skinheads

I know who have worked hard all their lives, would give you the coat off their back and do anything for you if you're considered "one of them". So, while this book is not to necessarily paint a rose-tinted picture as such, I hope this will educate those that have these misconceptions about skinheads. Here I hope to represent a real overview of the skinhead culture as a whole and to give real skinheads a voice, enabling them to tell their stories of how and why they became a skinhead and some of their most memorable experiences (good and bad) since becoming one. Some stories will inform you what it's like to be a real skinhead, while some will shock, and a few contradicting what is (or at least SHOULD be) at the heart and soul of being a skinhead. I also wanted to focus on many of the stories that have appeared in the press over the years. My main purpose here is to tell the truth and let you judge for yourselves and I certainly hope after reading the book that I've managed to give some people the heads-up and change their stereotypical view of skinheads.

Ian Phillips
January 2016

Skins Oxblood, Sweat and Beers

The Dawn of the Skinhead

"I used to have to run and hide from the skinheads as I was sure to get a kicking if they caught me." DJP (a 16-year-old black West Indian) from Liverpool

"I clearly remember black as well as white skinheads all together...they (skinheads) used to knock at the door to see if my older brother had got any new reggae records." RS (a mixed race teenager) from London

'Britain first became aware of the term Paki-bashing last Wednesday. A group of skinheads boasted on TV that they beat up coloured immigrants in East London for the fun of it.' *Sunday Mirror*, 1969

"The police don't like the boots. They take them off us at football matches; we get picked on all the time. Just walk along the street in boots and they'll stop you." David Ward, Skinhead

"I see them everywhere - racing along the aisles of local trains, wrestling on escalators, hanging around country towns, throwing stones on television."

"I remember walking to Cubs aged about nine in the late sixties. My route took me down a long alley and one night there was a gang of skinheads in front of me. I hung back and one of them spotted me and started taking the mickey, saluting and shouting dib-dib-dib. Then they realised they were scaring me and their attitude changed completely. They ushered me past them, and sent me on my way with some friendly reassurances. It was an important early lesson that you can't necessarily judge by appearances." Neil Hoskins, Aylesbury, UK

15

"They act as the shock troops of the age revolution, mercenaries who will attack any minority group just for fun - Catholics, Pakistanis, courting couples, police, pop groups, football crowds. Invisible and unpredictable, they are given respectable excuses for vandalism by adults..."

Back in nineteenth-century England in the north-west there had been youth groups with their own dress codes who were referred to as Scuttlers. However, it wasn't until the late 1940s, following the second World War, when Saville Row Tailors attempted to revive the styles and fashions of King Edward VII's reign between 1901 – 1910, known as the Edwardian era, that the first distinctive youth style and subculture made its first appearance. In London some of the working-class youths would wear long Edwardian coats, fancy waistcoats and tight-fitted trousers, have greased-back hairstyles that bore quiffs and DAs conspicuously placed. They went to great lengths to appear as a group that was totally separated from ordinary, conventional lifestyles. This subculture group was first known as Cosh Boys and rapidly spread across the UK. In 1953 an article in *Daily Express* ran with a headline that shortened Edwardian to Teddy and, from there on, the Cosh Boys became more commonly known as Teddy Boys.

1956 the American film *Blackboard Jungle* marked a watershed in the UK. The film incorporated social commentary into its plot that was set in an inter-racial, inner-city school, adapted from the novel of the same name by Evan Hunter and directed by Richard Brooks. As well as being remembered for a memorable performance by future Oscar winner Sidney Poitier as a rebellious student, it's also highly regarded for its innovative use of rock and roll in its soundtrack. The film truly marked the rock and roll revolution, which included the legendary hit 'Rock Around The Clock' by Bill Haley & His Comets. When the film was shown in the Elephant and Castle, the teenage Teddy Boys would riot, tearing up the seats and dancing in the aisles, and subsequent screenings at cinemas across the UK would see even more riots occur.

The Teddy Boys soon gained notoriety for violent clashes with rival gangs, often which made headlines in the press (though the media often exaggerated and sensationalized such stories). The most notable event took place in 1958 with the infamous Notting Hill race riots where several Teddy Boys were implicated in attacks on the West Indian community.

It was the 1950s that saw nearly half a million blacks and Asians migrate to Britain in desperate search of a better life. The long post-war economic boom had been fuelled by the reconstruction and American investment which had led to the creation of several substantial immigrant communities in the majority of the West European countries. The war had played a major part in stimulating migration. In Britain the expansion of the Merchant Navy, the mobilization of people in the armed forces and the harnessing of industry and agriculture for the war sparked serious labour shortages. These were only partially met by women, young people and Irish workers. So Colonial workers were eagerly recruited and brought to Britain, some even coming voluntarily. Many of these immigrants filled these labour requirements in

London's hospitals, transportation venues and railway developments. However, many black and Asian immigrants were often subject to racism, prejudice and violence. Yet it was the immigrants that many frowned upon that had largely helped the rebuilding of the post-war urban London economy.

By the late 1950s the economy in Britain was booming. This inevitably led to a far higher increase in disposable income for many young people. Many youths chose to spend their money on clothing, particularly new fashions that had been largely popularised by American soul groups, British R&B bands and clothing merchants in Carnaby Street. Their look was sharp and smart, often dressed in tailored suits, and they would soon become widely known as Mods. Of course, some had more disposable income than others, and those with lesser means would make do with practical clothing that reflected their lifestyle and employment. These included work boots or army boots, Sta-prest trousers or straight-leg jeans, braces (which were referred to as suspenders in North America) and button down shirts. Whenever possible, the Mods would congregate at dancehalls, where they would enjoy amphetamine-fuelled nights dancing away to soul, ska, bluebeat and rocksteady music.

The mods and the rockers had all but succeeded the Teddy Boys by the dawn of the 1960s. The Mods rode on Vespas and Lambrettas, decorating their scooters with artificial fur fabric and other accessories. They bought the finest Italian suits and considered themselves elite. In opposition to the Mods were the Rockers, who wore leather jackets and rode heavy motorbikes, largely influenced by the American Hell's Angels. These two conflicting subcultures often were the subject of the media, instilling fear for many and quickly leading to them being labelled as 'folk devils'.

The mods and the rockers (or 'greasers' as they were known by some) became notorious for their brawls, often occurring on bank-holiday weekends around Southern

England's seaside town resorts such as Brighton, Margate, Bournemouth and Clacton. Mods would sometimes sew fish hooks or razor blades into the backs of their lapels in order to shred the fingers of assailants (something that the Teddy Boys, too, had often done). Other weapons favoured by the mods were bike chains, coshes and flick knives.

The conflict between these two subcultures came to a head during Whitsun weekend of 18 and 19 May 1964, where many Londoners headed for the seaside resorts for their holiday. Thousands upon thousands of both mods and rockers descended upon Margate, Brighton and Broadstairs, and within moments began openly fighting, many using deckchairs as weapons. The worst violence was in Brighton, the fights lasting two days and moving along the coast to Hastings and back. This was tagged by the media as the 'Second Battle of Hastings'. A small group of rockers were isolated on Brighton beach and even in spite of being protected by the police, the number of mods became overwhelming and each found themselves violently assaulted. Once calm had been restored the court judge imposed heavy fines on many of the offenders, describing those that had been arrested as 'Sawdust Caesars'.

In his study *Folk Devils and Moral Panics,* sociologist Stanley Cohen examined the extensive media coverage of these mods and rockers riots in the mid-1960s, leading him to the term 'moral panic'. This term was defined in the Oxford University's Dictionary of Sociology as, 'The process of arousing social concern over an issue – usually the work of moral entrepreneurs and the mass media.' Cohen argued the point that, even though there had been many riots between the mods and rockers, these events were really no different to the many evening brawls that occurred between youths in the 1950s and early 1960s, both usually taking place after football games and at seaside resorts. He also goes on to point out that the UK media had turned the whole mod culture into a negative symbol of delinquent and deviant status.

Interestingly, following an article in the *Independent* which reflected on the Margate riots in the 60s, a reader commented: 'A lot of the fighting in the 60s was set up by the press so they could get good copy. They would pay mods and rockers a fiver or so each to bundle and then take photos which would then be released in the press with tag lines such as 'the violent youth of today'. I know this is true because some of the journalists from back then have admitted it. Also any REAL fighting was more of a tribal thing between different groups, as was the football violence, not mindless thuggery and looting...All this crappy romanticising of the 60s culture really has got to stop because it just perpetuates the myths and lies that become 'fact'. Oh, by the way, I was around then and my uncle lived just down the road from Margate, which we used to visit on a regular basis.'

By 1966 there had become a considerable divide between the smooth mods (also widely referred to as the peacock mods), who were considerably less violent and always wore the latest and most expensive clothes, and the hard mods (also known by many as gang mods, lemonheads and peanuts). The hard mods had a more working-class image and could be readily identified by their shorter, often cropped, hair. By around 1968 these hard mods had become more commonly known as skinheads, although other nicknames for them at that time included Noheads, baldheads, cropheads, suedeheads, prickles, and boiled eggs. An original mod from the sixties, John Waters, once recalled on the *Modculture* website: "There were two distinct types of mod within the London area. The first was the familiar scooter boys which have become the generally accepted face of Sixties' Modernism. However, there was another type of mod back in those days. These were the members of the many mod 'firms'...members of these gangs would not be seen dead on a scooter, their preferred mode of transport being a car. They were meticulous in their dress, the order of the day being the mohair suit, velvet-collar overcoats and, as often as not, a 'Blue Beat' hat."

It wasn't until 1969 that Skinheads became their common name and, even as late as 1970, some still would refer to them as hard mods. It has been suggested that short hair was more practical for these working-class youths in their industrial jobs, as well as in street fights. Renowned fashion photographer Iain McKell, who made his name in the seventies and eighties through shooting skinheads, new romantics and Madonna's very first magazine cover, once recalled his memory of the skinheads from around this era:

"I remember the skinheads the first time around, in 1969, when it was really hard-core. I must have been 12 or 13 and I was in a cafe in Bristol when this bloke walked in, hair cropped, Ben Sherman shirt, braces, Levi's, and DM boots. Then another one...and another one. And I thought, 'Hang on a minute, there's something going on here, this is a scene, there's some kind of code.' And in those days, it was shocking to see something like that."

It was also something of a defiance against the more middle-class, long-haired hippies. 1967 had seen the so-called Summer of Love. As the mod scene was slowly fading, it seemed at one point that the only British youth subculture that was thriving was hippy communes and student marches. This mainly consisted of middle-class youths dressed in flamboyant flares and flowers set against a kaleidoscope of psychedelia and Paisley patterns. They smoked weed, took LSD and went around spouting superficial babble about love and peace in the world. The skinheads mainly despised the hippies for being drop-outs, as they were working-class and certainly never had the privilege of taking any 'time out', most having gone straight from school into work, where they worked long hours for little pay. One 16-year-old skinhead stated, rather bluntly, in

1968, that he was against "Long hair, pop, hippy sit-ins, live-ins, and the long-haired cult of non-violence."

The skinheads (still largely known as hard mods/peanuts) crashed a hippy gathering in Grosvenor Square in October 1968. As the hippies chanted "Victory to the NLF (National Liberation Front)" and "Ho Ho Ho Chi Minh", the skins began shouting "Student students Ha Ha Ha". Just a month prior to this, the *Daily Telegraph* had run an article on skinheads regarding another incident:

'Hundreds of youths in hob-nailed boots left Margate last night after a weekend of fights and scuffles with police. The boot brigade, successors to the mods and rockers, met police in several clashes on the seafront yesterday and on Sunday. One boy, sixteen and dressed in a hill-billy fashion in heavy brown boots and jeans held up by braces said,

"These boots are just part of the uniform. They make us look hard."'

Photo © Ross Fergus Croft

Fights with Hells Angels would become the norm as an original skinhead, David Ward, once recalled in a magazine article: "We look nicer, but we're much rougher than the Angels. They're always saying how brave they are, but we think they go in more for beating up old ladies than fighting tough people like us. At football matches the 'Cock of the Tilton' – the best scrapper at the Tilton Road entrance – is a Skinhead. We usually chase the Angels into town and scrap with them there. We always start it. I don't know why we fight; it's just that every time you see an Angel you've got to. You must do what everybody else does. We're not organised with financial accounts and everything like the Angels – we're just a gang of mates who know each other. There are thousands of us around; particularly in this area. Parents don't have the faintest idea what goes on. When they heard about the fighting, my parents started to get a bit stroppy, but I'd threatened I'd leave home if they didn't stop nagging. So now I've got them where I want them, and I do as I like."

More often than not, the word Skinhead would quickly be used in a negative context in the media, many using it as a terminology to represent hooliganism. Even the Prime Minister of the time, Harold Wilson, said when speaking in Parliament in 1969 that certain Tory rivals were 'the skinheads of Surbiton'. Contrary to this misconception, any skinhead from that era will be keen to point out how much they respected older people, loved their country, loved themselves and loved their mums!

At the dawn of the UK's Skinhead movement, politics did not play any part in the scene. The subculture originated amongst working class youths and was like a symbol of working class pride. While retaining many mod influences, the look of the original skinhead was greatly influenced by West Indian (mainly Jamaican) rude boys, not only in terms of fashion but also the music, which varied between ska, rocksteady and early reggae (prior to the tempo being slowed down and the lyrics focusing on black nationalism and the Rastafari movement).

As the 1960s were coming to an end, the era of the Skinheads was booming and soon became a media fascination. One of the first writers to notice this new phenomenon (albeit not in the most positive way) was Chris Welch, who wrote in the pop press at the time, 'It's a curious thing that whenever...a pillar of our bewildered society wants to cast stones, they instantly talk about long-haired louts/yobs/hippies/students etc...Yet anybody who had ventured on the streets will instinctively know that they have nothing to fear from the long-haired youth who merely wants to turn on in peace to his favourite band and chick. The sight of cropped heads and the sound of heavy boots entering the midnight wimpy bar or dance hall is the real cause for sinking feelings in the stomach'. And just as the rockers had proved to be the enemy of the mod, the middle-class student drop-outs became an early target of the skinheads.

A particularly disparaging article was written about the skinheads in 1972 in a book called *Rock File*, written by Pete Fowler and edited by Charlie Gillett:

'The Skinheads came from the same areas that had witnessed the rise of the Mods – the East End of London and the outer rings of Suburbs. But whereas the Mod had seen his 'enemy' as the Rocker, and had rationalised his life style accordingly (Cleanliness vs. Grease; Scooter vs. Motor Bike; Pills vs. Booze), the new Skinheads reacted against the Hippies. Their hair was short to the point of absurdity, they were tough and went around in their 'bovver boots' for the express purpose of beating hell out of any deviants, and they wore braces. Braces! For God's sake, some sort of weird throwback to the thirties.

'At Hyde Park in July 1969, they showed their strength. According to Geoffrey Cannon's report on the event, a free concert was given by the Rolling Stones. It was 'A Nice Day in the Park'. It was things 'nice' that the Skins objected to.

John Peel and the other beautiful people saw everything as being 'really nice' – the Skins wanted others to see them as really horrible.

'The concert was odd. Here were the Rolling Stones, the old Mod idols, being defended by Hells Angels, the descendants of the old Rockers, and the whole scene was laughed at by the new skinheads, who were the true descendants of the old Mods. After all, it seems likely that most of their elder brothers and sisters had spent their teens down Soho getting blocked on a Saturday night. The wheel had come full circle.'

Of the same concert mentioned in that less-than-flattering article, a story was written about this in the 'underground' magazine *International Times* (often referred to as IT) in January 1970, where a section was entitled YELL, which was made by skinheads for skinheads (covering topics of their choices such as Skinhead fashion, music etc.). Here the YELL crew said in reference to that Hyde Park concert:

"'DISGUSTING': That's one word for us, according to people who write in to us and IT. Neil, of Kennington, asks us 'If you get bored with hairy music, what the fuck are you doing at Hyde Park anyway?' Well, Neil, seeing as you go on to say that you try to see our point of view, we think we can tell you the obvious answer. We go there because there is nothing else to do, because it is free, because it is better than nothing. But there could be something better for us, because we're human too. Quite a lot of the Hyde Park music seems pseudo to us, true, but you've got your taste, we've got ours...'

That certainly answered the question put to the Skinheads who had attended the concert in the summer of 1969! Straight to the point, admittedly a little bold, but, on the contrary, you couldn't have gotten a more honest answer!

Skinheads detested any form of authority as one East End skinhead stated in *The Paint House* book: "Everywhere there are fucking bosses...they're always trying to tell us what to do...don't matter what you do, where you go, they're always there. People in authority, the people who tell you what to do and make sure you do it. It's the system we live in; it's the governors' system." How time hasn't changed!

Attitudes against authority figures were hardly confined to just skinheads, with it being like that with other working class youths. Mothers actually welcomed the short hair, mainly because it presented less problems than long hair. Fathers usually liked the style because it was neat and very workmanlike.

With the skinhead look having been largely borrowed from the Jamaican rude boys, and with their mutual love of reggae music, there was an increasing liaison between the young West Indians and young white skinheads in many London districts and, in particular, Birmingham. An article that was featured in *Black Music* magazine in 1974, with the heading *Reggae Underground,* spoke of the camaraderie between early skinheads and blacks:

White kids had been associating with blacks in clubs like the Ram Jam since black music first became popular in England, but it wasn't until 1967 that the whites had begun to appreciate reggae music and to mimic the black lifestyle. They fell in love with the first wave of reggae music that Pama records issued, like the instrumentals - 'Spoogy', 'Reggae on Broadway' and '1000 tons of Megaton' by Lester Sterling. They stomped to the frantic dance records like 'Work it' by the Viceroys and 'Children Get Ready' by the Versatiles. They sang along to Pat Kelly's 'How Long will it Take' and Slim Smith's 'Everybody Needs Loves' and laughed at rude items like Max Romeo's 'Wet Dream' or Lloyd Tyrell's 'Bang Bang Lulu'

Pretty soon you couldn't go to a black house party without finding a gang of skinheads but amazingly there was very little black/white violence and hardly any resentment. Black and white youth have never been as close as they were in the skinhead era despite the 'mixing' in the trendier soul scenes nowadays. The skinheads copied the way we dressed, spoke, walked, the way we danced. They danced with our chicks, smoked our spliffs and ate our food and bought our records.

Any racism that existed was aimed at Pakistanis, many of whom lived in areas where there was virtually no integration. Again, the propaganda of the media would have you believe that every single skinhead was solely responsible for attacks on the Asian community. The media soon began sensationalising stories on skinhead's activities known as "Grease-bashing", "Squaddie-bashing", and "Queer-bashing". Many Asians had migrated to Britain in the late 1960s and both blacks and whites within skinhead gangs felt threatened by these immigrants and swiftly targeted them. This victimisation was fuelled further by the politician Enoch Powell's 'River of blood' speech, where he openly criticised both Commonwealth immigration and the anti-discrimination legislation proposed in the UK. Powell was totally opposed to the mass influx of Asians to Britain, calling for repatriation of all immigrants. His speech made such comments as "In this country in 15 or 20 years' time the black man will have the hand over the whip man...We must be mad, literally mad, as a nation to be permitting the annual flow of 50,000 dependants...It is like watching a nation busily engaged in heading up its own funeral pyre."

In *Subculture – The Meaning Of Style* by Dick Hebdige in 1979, he wrote '*The phenomena of Paki-bashing by both white skinheads and blacks alike is explained as 'A displacement manoeuvre whereby the fear and anxiety produced by limited identification with one black group is transformed into aggression against another.'*

With regards to "Paki-bashing", a long-standing Skinhead is quoted in an article in IT magazine in 1972: "I'll tell you why I hate the bloody Pakis. I'll tell you a story. A week or so ago I was walking down the street with a couple of mates. I wanted a light for my fag, so I walk up to this Paki git and ask him, "You got a light, mate?" And what do you think the fucker did? I'll tell you. He walks – no, runs – into this shop and buys me a box of matches! Now, I ask you! What the fuck could I with a bleeder like that but hit him? And another thing: have you ever been to their restaurants? Have you seen the way they grovel round you, the way they're always trying to please you? I hate them, that's all."

In that same article, the writer attempts to analyse this hatred, stating:' The logic of their hatred is this: the West Indian kids are mixing, and their influence is taking hold. They are beginning to see this country as their home. The Indians and the Pakistanis keep themselves to themselves and in Birmingham interaction between white working class and Asian is non-existent. To put it another way, the Indians and the Pakistanis are aspiring (if they are aspiring towards anything whilst they're living here) towards a middle-class set of values. They dress in carefully tailored suits, they are polite, and they are nice. The West Indian kids, on the other hand, are more 'normal' in the Skin's eyes. They get drunk, they like dressing up in Skin gear. They are willing to join forces.'

Yet the relationship between blacks and whites was never clear cut either. One skinhead would recall:

"Yes, we did have trouble with the blacks. I mean, there was a club that started up at Mile End that was called 'The A-Train' and yeah, sure, every Friday night, every Saturday night, whenever we chose to go up there, we'd have a battle with the blacks. But we had black guys on our side as well, a few coloured guys who'd stand behind you and fight for you as a brother, no problem".

An original Skinhead from this era vehemently denied any such racism, putting this point of view across: "For starters, most skinheads listened to Ska music which originated from Jamaica and was then created here in some of the first multi-cultural bands this country had seen. It's nonsense to tar them all with the same 'racist' brush. Yes, there are elements of the skinhead 'fashion' who went on to become right-wing racists, but that is true of every social group in this country. You wouldn't say "Ah, people from the countryside. The good old days of slavery and servitude", and nor should you do the same about skinheads, which is, in itself, racist."

Ricardo Scott, now a father and road worker, told the *Guardian* in 2011 when reflecting on his skinhead days in his youth: "The best sight [in those days] was a load of skinheads walking down the road. At that age, you would start to put fear into people and enjoy it when people got out the way. There was a lot of violence, which was there whether you wanted it or not. But that was the time, wasn't it? When you look back, you think it was stupid, but you are older now."

Other Skinheads may strongly disagree with the above statement; many who I've interviewed emphasising that it wasn't about violence, but more the sense of belonging and brotherhood, a strong passion for ska, reggae, rocksteady and soul music, music which had helped bring black and white people together. A Skinhead commented: "I was an original skinhead in the 70s in London. Our whole life revolved around reggae. We were not racist oriented. We were no angels; football violence, and kicking the shit out of Teds at Brighton and Southend was the norm. We were about, music, drinking, girls, and just having fun. Our entire music culture was black, for God's sake. I had many black skinhead friends."

A skinhead from Tipton also once commented, "I was hanging about with a black (West Indian) girl at the time that I'd met at a reggae night in West Brom and I never heard any racist comments from fellow skins at that time. Any hassle you had was from older white guys on a bus for example, pissed up, would see me with her and may get mouthy and vice versa if it was older West Indians and then they'd say something to her, or if we were in one of the reggae clubs in Handsworth, now and again someone got their 'arse in their hand' about us being together. But in our own area of Tipton I don't remember any racist incidents really, either with West Indians or Asians; I was just passionate about the music."

George Marshall, author of *Spirit of 69/A Skinhead Bible*, put it in a more succinct way: "'Pride not Prejudice' means being proud of the cult, the way you look, where you come from, your town, your country," Marshall explains. "Most skinheads are working class. You should take pride in that; you're as good as anybody else. But no prejudice, because people from other countries have got the right to be the same. So we're proud to be skinheads, but we're not prejudiced against anybody else."

Although skinheads were not primarily responsible for football violence, some played a prominent role in it where it became just the norm. Photographer Iain McKell, a public schoolboy with working-class parents, admitted he was mesmerised by the skinheads' defiance and aggression and he too wanted to become part of the scene. Recalling his memories at one particular football match, he commented,

"This big firm of lairy skinheads would stand behind the goal at Bristol City's ground, so one day I joined them, just to experience this feeling, this roar. They'd bang their boots against the corrugated tin wall behind them, and then they'd surge forward in this big wave."

As football was regarded as a battle, this meant the use of weapons for many. At first, the steel toecaps of industrial boots were seen as effective ways of fighting their opponents. These were later banned by the police, especially as some would weld steel spikes onto the toecaps. For example, the 'Millwall brick' was a newspaper that was folded several times and squashed together to form a cosh. Metal combs that bore sharpened handles were another prime example of how weapons could be made from objects which wouldn't immediately gain attention from the police. Then there were metal studded watch straps, sharpened coins, and Kung Fu stars with the edges filed down. In 1969, dart throwing became the norm, while rice flails, which were never permitted to be taken into football matches, were used in street battles, just as the edges of razor blades taped into the inside of fingers or inside boots were. Secret pockets were often sewn into the lining of coats in order to conceal weapons. Midland supporters even took to wearing metal pit helmets, the peaks sharpened to ensure a cutting edge. Another weapon used, but relatively minor in comparison to others, was the use of the aerosol paint can. "Tottenham Skins Rule, OK?" was often sprayed on nearly every available surface in a Northern town and was seen as a good way of annoying the enemy and celebrating your power.

When police began eventually confiscating skins' bootlaces, and in some cases their braces, the reaction of the skinhead was to then use a short wire to replace the laces in a way which could not be readily seen by the police.

However, it's important to note here that such statements can't be generalised, nor can you tar everyone with the same brush, and not all skinheads were involved in football violence, nor can the blame be squarely placed on the shoulders of skinheads. An interesting article published in the early 1970s saw two original skinheads being interviewed about how they saw themselves and their violence. Both belonged to different gangs, one in Islington, the other in Archway. Len Warrington had by then left the skinhead cult and was working for a printer in a display firm in Holloway:

"'I've still got my boots. I only wear them when I go to football. Up the Arsenal. They're not skinheads there though. When I was with the skinheads we wore shirts with a pleat in the back, Levis and boots. It was like being in the army. We all wore the same.

The younger ones now, like brothers, go out and if they get into bother they call on you. My younger brother, he's thirteen, goes around in a gang, they meet after school and walk about the streets. He wears flares and tries to get the stuff we used to wear. I still like reggae but he goes on about underground music.

I miss the bother in one way. You'd get another crowd walking towards you and you got that feeling that you knew they wouldn't move away. I used to like that.

The only bother now is up football with the other fans. Last season, the worst lot were West Ham. Even if we win or lose we still go out and meet the others. I don't know why we do it - it's just like something after a football match. Probably the excitement or something that makes you do it. You don't think about anything much when you're fighting, just that you don't get your face kicked in."

The other skinhead interviewed for this same article was Alan Timms who also worked for the same firm as Len's. He, too, had left the Skinhead scene by the time of this article:

"I became a skinhead for the fashion and something to do each night. It was only a fashion. I mean I wear flared trousers now - got rid of me Crombie. I've changed considerably. For a start I've been courting strongly for about fourteen months and lost contact with a lot of my friends. You just grow up, I suppose. I still see my gang, but I don't go around with them as much. Like my girl, she was part of the gang then, just followed on. It was always bother coming to you or you going to bother in those days.

I belong to the Archway Club and there you are free to wear what you like. We go to the club three nights a week and we just enjoy ourselves, we hardly ever get any bother. There used to be lots of fights then, of course. Some of them were very bad, fifty geezers involved in one, you know. I don't go out looking for trouble now: the only time is when I see someone getting the better of another geezer."

Some skinheads were renowned for unprovoked attacks. In Brighton during the Easter bank holiday in 1970, a report of an incident was published in the *Daily Mail*:

"A group of skinheads trapped a man behind a parked car. They attacked him with boots and fists. The man had done them no harm. He was merely walking in the street when they arrived. He is a victim - like so many others in this year when law and order is a topical issue - of unprovoked aggression. But this time there was someone to put it on record."

Photographer Bill Cross, who worked for the newspaper, stated: 'I was in Pavilion Gardens, 200 yards from the front, when I saw about 200 skinheads running through the street shouting football slogans. They started off in a sort of jog-trot which became faster and faster. As they increased speed they shouted louder. It was mass hysteria. Two men aged between 20 and 25 were walking through the gardens as the mob ran forward. They were just ordinary chaps, not wearing leather jackets or anything like that. About seven or eight of the leading skinheads started kicking at them. The two men held out their arms trying to reason with the skinheads who were shouting at the top of their voices. The skinheads took no notice. One of the attacked men ran out of my camera frame and was chased by two skinheads. The rest set about another chap as he tried to escape behind a parked car. They kicked and punched him and then ran to catch up with the main body. The skinheads broke windows of shops and overturned tables outside restaurants. They held their arms in the air like victorious gladiators. I couldn't help feeling a bit sick watching parents grabbing their children from the gang's path.'

At the end of the day, there are no excuses for such actions, but not all skinheads were bad; some went on to be highly successful. The media, on the other hand, saw them as all being alike. The following dialogue from a skinhead perhaps demonstrates the exact skinhead psyche:

"I went to college. I'm an electrician by trade, and touch wood, I've never been unemployed. You know, several others who were in our gang are in business now. One of them is an architect surveyor with a half-million pound turnover and two villas in Spain. He got done for having a row at Coventry, I remember. He got three months D.C. (Detention Centre) for steaming into the Old Bill with a hammer.

"All these things what we was to the older people - hooligans, louts, tearaways - you know, it's not true. I mean I like to think I'm a likeable person as such. Maybe I wasn't so much then, but even then I was polite and never disrespectful to elderly people. I had neighbours who'd say 'Oh he's a lovely boy, he helped me home with my shopping yesterday,' and all that. I mean, just because I done things on Saturday afternoon on the terraces and Friday night at the club, it doesn't make me a bad person."

The Fashion of the Skinhead

"In 1970 we wore the Doc Martins with Levi's + half inch turn up, Ben Shermans and Harringtons or Crombie overcoats. If we were going out to a dance we would wear Sta-prest 2 tone trousers with Brogues and white socks and always clip on braces. Hair was a grade 3 crew-cut but not bald like you see skinheads today. We loved Reggae music and had special dances we stomped to, some of our mates were West Indian black guys, and we all just mixed up together. Back between 1969 - 1971 we certainly did all look the same and if you were on the street and another group of skins came along they would call out 'SKINHEAD' in a type of football hooligan voice. I remember masses of us at football matches and the police had a hard time trying to keep us under control, it was a bit like an army - a time I will never forget."

"In the late 60s I wore two-tone tonic suits, Levi 501s, Sta-prest, and Ben Shermans. My hair was short with longer bits at the bottom.... Loved blue beat and ska and reggae...We had certain dances we would do in lines e.g. the moon stomp was great! You had to go out with the boys from your area, otherwise there would be a fight if you were with a lad from another town... I wore braces too at times, and a tin pin in your Crombie was important..."

"I remember going out and getting my longish Mod style hair shaved off in 1969 (I was only 13) and my Ma decided to lock me in my bedroom until it grew back again! She's still trying to do it now, and I'm in my fifties!! Great fashions at the time, I remember having hob nail boots and a donkey jacket (very fashionable).

Also made-to-measure suits from Burtons. I still like to dress the same way now (when allowed by the wife!!)."

"I remember going to Great Yarmouth 69 in the back of my dad's car and Skinheads were everywhere. I thought I was going to dress like that. My old man said, "If you come in with a pair of those boots they will go on the fire". I was 11. I started High School that year and took a job in a car wash. First thing I bought was a pair of Doc Martins boots, cherry red. I never looked back. I joined a local Gang on a sprawling council estate in Luton and still see my old mates. I only wear Royal Brogues and a real velvet collar Crombie. £460- Ouch! My misses says: once a Skinhead, always a Skinhead. Keep the faith."

"I'm a skinhead 60s girl. Trevira mohair tonic suits, Sta-prest, Ben Shermans and the sheepskin coat. We were from Ilford and danced at the Ilford Palais on Saturday afternoons. 'Al Capone' was huge! I wore "granny shoes" from Anello and David on Tottenham Court Road in matching colours to suits. I'm 55 now and can never forget those fantastic days. I am now a DJ and still enjoying all the Tighten Up stuff! I loved the feather-cut cropped hair back then!"

"The skinhead fashion was a natural transgression from the mods era arriving in the East End of London 1968-69. My first-ever recollection of seeing skinheads was in London in the summer of 1969 on a visit to Wembley to see my local team North Shields in the amateur cup as a skinny 15 year old!"

The fashion of the early skinheads would usually include donkey jackets, army greens, working jeans, industrial boots and braces. Highly polished steel toe-capped boots would become like a badge of identity and pride, as well as a useful weapon, though eventually they were banned at football matches. In suggesting all skinheads are racist is a stark contradiction in itself, as whites and blacks happily socialised together at dance halls and clubs, all sharing a mutual interest and love of dancing and music. Much of the skinhead style had been emulated from the hip, young West Indians of many inner-city areas such as Brixton and Lambeth. These black youths were known as Rude Boys or Rudies. They could often be seen hanging around street corners in Brixton, dressed in long black coats, which would later become the Crombies of the skinheads, trousers that revealed white socks, and flat black shoes. Their cool style and exuberance in dance halls garnered admiration and respect from their white contemporaries.

Photo © Stewart Home

Although the most common image which springs to mind when thinking of the typical skinhead look is boots and braces, their style would switch in the evening when going to dance halls and clubs. Skinhead suits were vastly similar to those worn by the mods. While in the daytime the look was loose and hard wearing, clothes worn by the skinheads were tailored and expensive. The most highly revered suits by Dormeuil included a petrol blue and red two-tone suit or a fine mohair suit. The sole aim was to out-dress everyone else at the dance hall. Ties and tiepins set off the expensive suits, while silk handkerchiefs that were secured with studs were worn in the breast pockets of suits and Crombies.

Photo © Dave Ealand and Jason Hughes

The skinhead style soon rapidly spread through the football clubs, clubs and dance halls and had been firmly established long before the media had gotten hold of it. The supporters of London clubs such as Chelsea, West Ham, and Tottenham included several skinheads and not before long they made their presence felt, their appearance becoming distinguishable to rival supporters. Ian Walker had once recalled seeing over 4,000 skinheads at a football match in 1968, noting that, "They all wore bleached Levis, Dr Martens, a short scarf tied cravat style, cropped hair. They looked like an army and, after the game, went into action like one."

The skinhead label stems from the fact that you can see the scalp, or skin, through very short hair. Although some argue that it was influenced by crew-cuts that were popular among the US armed forces, it is actually a totally different style altogether. The American army style crew-cuts called for hardly any hair at the back and sides and a shaven but longer top. In fact, the heads of the US military became so concerned that any of the servicemen posted in the UK would be mistakenly identified as skinheads, they allowed the men to wear wigs and hairpieces when off duty in 1969.

The majority of electric razors have different number settings, with grade one giving the shortest crop and number four (or sometimes five) being the longest. The settings chosen from a skinhead would vary from area to area. Usually if someone turned up at school with a number two, others would subsequently follow suit and emulate the style too. Baldness was never considered cool but some skinheads would adopt the look that was referred to as a "dark shadow", which was a razor cut without any of the attachments and so would therefore be even shorter than a grade one. The whole idea of having a skinhead was to look sharp, smart and tough. Other variations would include what West Indians called a skiffle, which was a shaved-in, pencil thin parting, which ran from the front to the crown and was traditionally on the left-hand side of the head. Sideburns were considered very fashionable as they made the skinheads look older and more streetwise. These were referred to as mutton chops, the look being led by Arsenal's Charlie George.

Doc Martens didn't really come into wide circulation until steel toe-capped boots had been banned from football matches. Prior to this, basically any pair of lace-up leather boots would be deemed acceptable, providing they looked the part. Some skinheads even took to wearing boots that were a few sizes too big for them, all to add to the bovver effect. But it was generally the steel toe-capped boots that were the most popular. The metal bit on these boots would be exposed and either painted white or painted in football colours to give an extra air of menace. There were some industrial boots you could get that had already been painted. The likes of National Coal Board miners' boots and army boots were fairly easy to find with eight or ten-hole boots being standard. When steelies (as they were referred to) were banned by the police at football matches, Doc Marten became the norm. Docs polished up well, better than most others in fact, and were far more comfortable to wear.

While trousers ranged from army greens to corduroys, jeans were easily the most popular in skinhead circles. Jeans would usually either be shortened or turned up to above the ankle in order to show off the boots. Levi's red tags were the jeans to be seen in, which had also proved hugely popular with the mods before them. Button flies were fashionable and 501s were made from far heavier denim compared to today. The heavier denim ensured the jeans had more longevity. Most red tag 501s came in a shrink-to-fit format, the idea being that you buy a pair one or two sizes too big, jumped in the bath with them on and hey- presto!--they would shrink to make a perfect fit. However, the trouble was that when they went through the washing machine, they'd often shrink again, leaving it very difficult to actually get into them. Then there was the blue dye that would rub into your legs and also mark the sides of the bathtub, which both would become a real task to remove. Levi's were really meant to be worn on the hip, but skinheads would pull them above the waist, hence the need for braces to help hold them up. Other jeans manufacturers popular at this time were Lee and Wrangler, particularly outside of London where Levi's were hard to acquire.

Shirts were the final touch to the skinhead uniform in 1969. In the early days of the skinheads, nearly any shirt would do, but gradually two styles became a firm favourite. These were either the collarless union shirt usually coming in plain colours or occasionally in stripes. The other was the classic American button-down, which had been favoured by the mods in the mid-sixties. Ben Sherman was the most popular maker of the button-down shirt, originally made from a comfortable Oxford woven cloth, with a button at the back of the collar, a back pleat and a back hoop designed for hanging the shirt up.

While Ben Shermans' were the most popular shirts, there were others that were worn by the style-conscious skinhead. Brutus offered a decent range of shirts as did Jaytex, who, it could be argued, offered the best range of checked shirts available on the market. Cherished by skinhead girls were the Permanent Press range, their button-down blouses being devoured. Famous golfer Arnold Palmer even endorsed his own brand of excellent button-downs. Decent shirts were in such high demand that local tailors soon began producing their own versions to see to the eager skinhead customer.

The Fred Perry short-sleeved shirts were also often sported by the skinheads. The advertising slogan for these shirts read, "Shirt by Fred, 'Nuff Said.", instilling confidence in the customer that you were getting a top-quality garment. Some of these were heavy, three or four buttons, while easily the most popular had piping on the collar and sleeves, and seemingly influenced by football colours (white and navy blue were for Spurs, claret and blue for West Ham etc.).

So the skinhead look was definitely the height of working-class fashion and gave any mod or city gent a run for their money. The tabloid headlines at the time always seem to centre on the boots and braces, completely oblivious to the fact that the skinheads were the most style conscious group of kids around. However, jeans and boots were put away when it came to the skinheads attending football matches, in favour of the Levi's Sta-Prest, the mohair suits and brogues that were polished to the max, complemented by equally impressive gear. The skinhead girls usually bore stylish feather-cuts and would wear skirts and stockings and slightly longer jackets. The alternate look for the skinhead girl would be keyhole backed mohair mini-dresses.

The Music of the Skinhead

"I want all you skinheads to get up on your feet, put your braces together and your boots on your feet and give me some of that old Moonstomping." Symarip

"Skins are just down-to-earth kids who at least work for a living. We wear boots and braces because we like them." Slade

"I don't like skinheads coming to my gigs. I LOVE skinheads coming to my gigs!" Laurel Aitken

"I can always remember going to fun fairs with my big brother and they always played ska music like Live Injection and Monkey Spanner. Not like the crap today. It was the same at football when the chants were the words to pop songs of the time. Whatever happened to all those great songs?" Martyn Sears, Sittingbourne skin.

For years, British radio stations often refused to play records by black American artists, which is ironic considering it was these artists who had stirred the early work of top British acts such as The Beatles, Dusty Springfield, and the Rolling Stones. Due to this rigid regime, many 'pirate' stations were formed that broadcasted the music people really wanted to hear. Motown artists, particularly The Supremes (led by Diana Ross), were an early favourite on such stations. This led to many listeners abandoning the BBC radio shows in favour of the pirate stations. Not surprisingly, the BBC began to loosen its unfair policy, and around the time of The Supremes' major breakthrough with 'Where Did Our Love Go', both the pirates and all major stations played black American music equally. Prior to the Civil Rights Law in 1964, Motown album covers would often bear sketches rather than the artists themselves; basically to try and disguise the fact that the artists were black in what was a white-dominated selling market.

Most youth cultures have a particular style of music that unify and identify group members. The Teddy Boys had rock & roll, which had been declared "the Devil's Music" by some

American clergy. The Mods favoured soul music, the sounds of Motown and beat music. Though many of the early skins loved soul and Motown, too, they needed another genre of music to separate them from other subcultures. And this they did, adopting the Jamaican music which many black communities across South East London had brought from their homeland. This was most popular with the Rude Boys.

Reggae and Ska music was seldom heard unless you had West Indian friends. In Jamaica this style of music was distinctly different to jazz, rhythm and blues and soul from North America. Bearing an exotic sound, punctuated by a simple, throbbing, echoing beat, one critic described it as, "So gummy that you could throw it against a wall and it would stick..." Known variously as ska, blue beat or rocksteady, it was collectively referred to as reggae. Reggae was mainly played by disc jockeys in the dance halls and back rooms of pubs in South East London and North West Kent, such as the Daylight Inn, the Three Turns, the Lord Palmerston and the Ram Jam club in Brixton. Though the Mods were fans of reggae, it was the skinheads that really adopted it as their own. While steady soul music was used to do some close dancing to, it was reggae that had really had the skinheads up and dancing.

In the UK, ska and reggae was played in discos with sound systems that would highlight the beat. Even though interest was predominantly in the music rather than the actual artist, DJs often would add a voice to formerly instrumental recordings, which then would be recorded again for the second version of the same record. This often led to two disc jockeys competing with each other in the clubs, where they would take turns to do their voice-overs on the discs.

At first, British radio stations and the music press gave reggae hardly any support, many disregarding it as "crude", "simple", and in some instances "yobbo music" because of its strong connection to the skinhead scene. Due to the lack of press coverage and radio airplay, most record retailers wouldn't stock it, culminating in it failing to chart altogether. The only two shows dedicated to reggae before its breakthrough were BBC Radio London's *Reggae Time* and Radio Birmingham's *Reggae Reggae*. It was labelled as "Minority Programming", which is ironic considering some

reggae singles were selling tens of thousands of copies.

So in order to hear the latest reggae, specialist reggae stockists (often relegated to just a single market stall) and dance halls became all the more important to the skinhead. The biggest name in skinhead reggae was Trojan, a label that had been formed by Island Records and the Beat & Commercial Company in 1968. Island had been involved in promoting Jamaican music for several years, which had culminated in a #2 hit for Millie in 1964 with 'My Boy Lollipop'. However, by 1968 Island's owner, Chris Blackwell, had grown more interested in making the label more rock-oriented with a roster of bands such as King Crimson, Free, and Fairport Convention. In order to achieve this, Island had to shake off its reputation as a predominately specialist minority label, so, with the exception of Jimmy Cliff, all of the label's reggae artists were dropped.

Even big hits like Desmond Dekker's 'Israelites', which had topped the British Singles Chart, had only become hits after months of exposure on the underground scene. By 1969 smaller venues were no longer able to hold the vast numbers who would turn out for a reggae dance. Soon, town halls and top nightclubs such as London's Flamingo and The Roaring Twenties turned into shrines for reggae lovers and many skinheads would fill the dance floor, to do a spot of skanking, a form of dancing which had originated at Jamaican dance halls.

For a brief period the British group Slade attempted to jump on the skinhead bandwagon in order to be perceived as relevant and cutting edge. These were white working-class kids from Wolverhampton in the West Midlands and were the first UK band to dress in working-class fashion. On the front cover of their debut album *Play It Loud* (issued on the Polydor label), the group were seen wearing boots and braces in true skinhead style. This was all propaganda, though, as none of the band were in fact real skinheads, and they had only adopted the image on the insistence of their manager. This turned out to actually work against the band, as being classed as skinheads, promoters were often too wary to book them in fear of potential trouble and fighting from skinheads in attendance. This phase in their career was short-lived and by the time they first hit the chart in 1971 they had all reverted to their long-hair and were on their way to becoming icons on the glam scene (Slade's name would become associated with the skinhead scene again in 1978 when they played at the Great British Music Festival, during which someone ended up being stabbed while The Jam were playing).

Trojan Records was an ideal establishment to progress Jamaican music beyond just the West Indian communities. Here, the more cheaply-produced Jamaican tracks would see the rough edges smoothed over by the addition of strings and, on occasions, whole choirs in an effort to make them commercially viable for the British market. A flood of cover versions of pop and soul hits were also issued by many reggae and ska artists in a bid to crack the mainstream, all of which helped the Trojan label score seventeen top twenty hits between 1969 and 1972. Even so, many releases remained only popular on the underground scene, particularly devoured by skinheads where names like Ken Boothe and Pat Kelly became just as familiar to the skinhead as more famous artists like Desmond Dekker and Jimmy Cliff.

Other than the Trojan label, the Pama label provided some of the top sounds in skinhead reggae. Formed in 1967, Pama aimed each of its releases at the ethnic market and the skinhead cult. The Trojan and Pama labels inevitably tried to outdo each other and led to some unscrupulous dealings where Jamaican producers would fly into London and often sign a deal with both labels for the same releases. This all came to a head in late 1969 when Trojan released Symarip's 'Skinhead Moonstomp' to beat off competition from Derrick Morgan's 'Moonhop' (based on soul duo Sam and Dave's 'I Thank You'), released on one of Pama's subsidiary labels, Crab. Bunny Lee had licensed Derrick Morgan's 'Seven Letters' to both Trojan's subsidiary label, Jackpot, and to Pama on the Crab label. When it looked certain that Derrick Morgan's 'Moonhop' was about to become their biggest hit, Trojan responded by rush-releasing an unaccredited version of it as 'Skinhead Moonstomp' by The Pyramids but released under the name Symarip. 'Skinhead Moonstomp' has since become a widely-acclaimed skinhead standard while Derrick Morgan's 'Moonhop' has been all-but-forgotten, bar from obscurants.

In fact, The Pyramids would often record under a number of aliases, some releases seeing them credited as The Alterations, The Bed Bugs and The Rough Riders. Eventually both the Trojan and the Pama labels would begin producing their own material in the UK, often employing the use of several white musicians and Jamaican vocalists who were either living in the UK or were on tour. Interestingly,

Laurel Aitken, one of Pama's biggest-selling artists and often hailed as the Godfather of Ska, once commented that he was often the only black person in the studio when recording tracks.

After the success of 'Skinhead Moonstomp', many acts cashed in on celebrating skinheads, including The Pyramids (released under the name Symarip) with classics like 'Skinhead Girl' and 'Skinhead Jamboree', Laurel Aitken with 'Skinhead Train' (on the Nu Beat label), Joe The Boss with 'Skinhead Revolt' (Joe), The Mohawks with 'Skinhead Shuffle' (Pama), 'Skinheads Don't Fear' and 'Skinhead Moondust' by the Hot Rod Allstars (Torpedo), Desmond Riley's 'Skinhead', 'A Message To You' (Downtown), and several others.

Reggae music themes usually were drawn from the ghettoes of Trenchtown, Jamaica. Toots & the Maytal's '54-46 - That's My Number', another skinhead standard, is a reference to a prisoner's number. Songs usually spoke of drink, injustice, drugs, and generally the underdog fighting back, although some were straight-forward love songs. Most popular songs with skinheads from this period (besides those already mentioned in this chapter) included 'El Casino Royale'– Lynn Tait, County Stick & The Jets (Amalgamated label), 'Catch The Beat'– the Pioneers (Amalgamated), 'Clint Eastwood'– The Upsetters (Upsetter), 'How Long Will It Take' – Pat Kelly (Pama), 'What A Fire' – Ethiopians (SirJJ), 'Jesse James' – Laurel Aitken, 'Better Must Come' – Delroy Wilson (Jackpot), 'Al Capone'– Prince Buster (Blue Beat), 'Return of Django' - The Upsetters (Upsetter), 'Double Barrel' - Dave & Ansel Collins (Techniques), 'Liquidator' - Harry J and the All Stars (Maxi Trojan), 'Young, Gifted & Black' - Bob & Marcia (Harry J Records), '007 Shanty Town' - Desmond Dekker (Beverley's Records), 'Wet Dream' - Max Romeo (Unity), 'Guns of Navarone' - The Skatellites (Trojan), 'Come Into My Parlour' - The Bleechers (Upsetter), and so many, many more.

Many skinheads became serious collectors of Jamaican music: They all knew which day fresh stock would arrive at the local reggae stores, and the latest releases would be something to impress your mates with. Much pride was placed in a record collection, so much so that even skinhead hero Judge Dread would go down to the actual docks with other sound system operators to buy the records straight off the boat! It became the norm to scratch the name of a song and artist off a single in order to prevent your mates from getting hold of the latest top sounds. This was an old trick borrowed from the sound systems wars of sixties Jamaica.

By the seventies, reggae had all but lost its way for many white kids as it began to largely focus on Jah, Rastafarianism and all things Africa. Rastafarianism was a mystical cult based on the extension of Haile Selassie to the throne of Ethiopia and, in essence, concerns the downfall of the white colonial races (Babylon). Dub reggae was the music of the Rastas, which bared a chunky, steady beat that was less suitable for dancing. It eventually became the main genre of music played by the sound systems, as its popularity increased among the young blacks who had abandoned skinhead reggae. Typical themes in dub reggae dealt with the overthrow of Babylon and were conspicuously hostile to white people. In dealing with spiritual entities such as Jah or with ganja (marihuana), this was no longer something skinheads could identify with.

It wouldn't be until the mid-1970s when Bob Marley broke through to the mainstream that reggae enjoyed a significant resurgence in popularity. Glam became the latest trend and soul had been largely superseded by funk and disco music. Little did white reggae star Judge Dread know that when he released his classic 'Bring Back The Skins' from his album *Last Of The Skinheads* (released via the Cactus label) that his wish would come true just a few short years later when the skinhead subculture was revived.

Several years later in 2011, Michael de Koningh, in an excellent article for *Record Collector* magazine titled *Boots, Braces, Boss Reggae*, listed the fifty most collectable skinhead reggae tracks, along with his personal description of each recording which I've included here. Now, of course, these things are all purely subjective, but it's a well-rounded list which I wanted to include here in this chapter, with the record label and catalogue number indicated in brackets:

50. 'Baff Boom' - The Tenors (Crab, Crab 26) 1969 "A rolling lazy rhythm with great vocals. In other words, an all-time gem from a Jamaican vocal group that never made a bad record."

49. 'Call 1143' - Count Machuki & the Sound Dimension (Bamboo Bam 4) 1969 "A Studio One JA production issued on its then-new UK outlet, Bamboo, with the great DJ Machuki chatting over the immortal Flats from master horn-man Roland Alphonso. The Pama and Trojan labels connected far more easily to skinheads, particularly the latter as their distribution network was country-wide, but there were some fantastic releases on Bamboo, even if they were harder to find then."

48. 'Queen of the World' - Lloyd & Claudette (Big Shot BI 456) 1970 "A great piece of solid UK reggae, though, like many great home-grown productions, it leans heavily on a Jamaican original - in this instance 'The Worm' by Lloyd Robinson."

47. 'Boss A Moon' - SS Binns (Escort ES 818) 1970 "Sonny Binns, Hammond genius of The Rudies, organs-up Derrick Morgan's 'Moon Hop' rhythm to great effect."

46. 'Loch Ness Monster' - King Horror (Grape GR 3007) 1969 "A London Laurel Aitken production aimed at the boot boys, with gruff mumbling and shrieks from calypso performer Lord Davey over a recut of Pat Kelly's immortal 'How Long' rhythm."

45. 'Japanese Invasion' - Rico (Bullet BU 407) 1969 "A stalwart of the UK reggae scene, trombone player Rico

Rodriguez trundles along on a typical '69 instrumental with the odd vocal interjection, quite likely from Dice the Boss. Exactly the sound loved by the original skins."

44. 'Skinhead Shuffle' - The Mohawks (Pama PM 798) 1970 "A pleasant reggae instrumental is the best that you can say for this UK-recorded 45 from the funky Champ chaps."

43. 'A Fist Full Of Dollars' - The Hot Rod All Stars (Torpedo TOR 19) 1970 "Here we have a stumbling attempt to recreate the sparse Upsetters sound (which was very popular at the time), with spoken cowboy references and one-finger organ. Made in London for the skins - who were probably unaware of the tune, or, indeed, the whole label. Resurrected from the bargain bins by the new bovver boys in the 90s."

42. 'Reggay City' - Val Bennett (Crab, Crab 6) 1969 "An early "reggay" tune from the much underrated saxman Val, who was responsible for the gritty R&B-style horn in The Upsetters' chartbusting 'Return of Django'."

41. 'Ware Fare' - Bubby Lee All Stars (Unity UN 552) 1970 "Produced at Randy's JA with the great Jackie Mittoo playing melodic organ lines - which are joined by a flute part - and vocal interjections from Bunny Lee's brother Donald Tony Lee. A smooth dancer of a 45. The title is meant to be 'War Fare'."

40. 'John Jones' - Rudy Mills (Big Shot BI 509) 1968 "John Jones was the son of a gun, so Rudy Mills tells us on this sprightly Jamaican-recorded 45, which must have been one of the most ear-catching intros of any reggae record. An all-time classic skin tune from '69, and as popular with the old 'uns as the new recruits."

39. 'Stagger Back' - Cannon Ball King (Gas, GAS 133) 1969 "Horn-man Karl Bryan, aka King Cannon, covers The Tennors' wonderful cut, 'Baff Boom' (No.50 in this list), in fine intro style."

38. 'Doctor Sappa Too' - The Sound Dimension (Bamboo BAM 5) 1969 "A bubbling Studio One gem

featuring a sharp little horn line and a chirpy DJ - and, like most Bamboo 45s, very hard to obtain back then unless you lived in the right place."

37. 'Bad Day at Black Rock/Fragile' - The Cimarron Kid (Reggae REG 3003) 1970 "Spaghetti Westerns were massive in Jamaica with many records reflecting this - and, in due course, the London arm of reggae picked-up on it, as proved by this rather lacklustre affair. The obligatory gruff sub-Clint Eastwood spoken vocal tells us what a bad day it was, with a jerky, very English-sounding track running underneath. The flip, 'Fragile', is a nice up-tempo instrumental and may well have sold the 45 far better if it had been flipped."

36. 'Phrases' - The Reggae Boys (Gas, GAS 141) 1970 "Don't watch that, watch this', sing Glen and Alva over the wonderful 'Ba Ba' rhythm (see below). Played back-to-back, the two 45s can fill a floor in a flash."

35. 'Ba Ba' - The Reggae Boys (Gas, GAS 135) 1969 "When they weren't The Upsetters or The Hippy Boys, Carlton and Aston Barrett, Alva 'Reggie' Lewis and Glen Adams recorded as The Reggae Boys. 'Ba Ba' has a great sticky rhythm with chanted vocals - just how the skins want them. A real dancer's delights."

34. 'Jump A Fire' - The Voiceroys (Viceroys) (Punch PH 3) 1969 "A great pumping Jamaican tune with strong group vocals making for dance floor action."

33. 'Professor in Action' - The Scientists (Amalgamated AMG 848) 1969 "Jamaican producer Joe Gibbs had his label name cloned by Trojan for the UK release of his work. The mere sight of the label sends many skins into mouth-frothing desire and this is one of the rarer 45s - and it's a good instrumental too."

32. 'Pussy Got Nine Life/Lick It Back' (Boss Sound) - Hot Rod All Stars (Torpedo TOR 1) 1970 "All the Hot Rod records sound almost the same, with simple lyrics, one-finger organ and tinny rhythms. This is just another couple

of aimed-at-skins sides which sold zilch at the time and only found favour decades later."

31. 'Another Scorcher' - The Tennors (Big Shot BI 517) 1969 "The original rhythm base to 'V Rocket' (no.6 below) and a scorcher of a tune recorded by George Murphy's vocal group The Tennors."

30. 'Sufferer' - The Kingstonians (Big Shot BI 508) 1968 "The vocal to 'Splash Down' (No.16 below). A magnificent piece of music with great lyrics telling of the hardships suffered in life, from one of the foremost skinhead reggae vocal trios. An unusual subject for a skinhead's record box."

29. 'Skinhead Train' - Laurel Aitken (Nu Beat NU 047) 1969 "Using the bass line of The Maytals' stomper '54-46', Mr Aitken gives the skinheads what they want. A solid moon-stomping 45, this is one of the easiest made-for-skinheads records for collectors to track down."

28. 'Spread Your Bed' - The Versatiles (Crab, CRAB 5) 1969 "Jump-up reggae of the highest order from another top-flight Jamaican vocal group loved by the '69 boys and still always in the DJ box 40-plus years later."

27. 'The Drifter' - Dennis Walks (Crab, CRAB 10) 1969 "One of the most versioned tracks in reggae and a great showcase for producer Harry Mudie, with sparkling brass and a smooth-but-tough rhythm over which Dennis tells us of his roaming life."

26. 'Sin Pon You' - Laurel Aitken (Ackee ACK 106) 1969 "The usual skinhead-centred stuff from Laurel, with the flip it being a bit on the rude side."

25. 'Moon Rock/Cut Up Munno' - Laurel Aitken (Bamboo BAM 16) 1970 "Laurel doing what he did best, using bouncy rhythms and aiming his vocals at skins. It seemed as if every other record was about the moon in 1970, obviously due to the Apollo landing the previous year. One of only a few non-Studio One productions to emerge from Bamboo."

24. 'Haunted House' - The Upsetters (Spinning Wheel SW 100) 1970 "Dave Barker's vocal cut of the classic 'Spinning Wheel' left plenty to be desired, but when Mr Perry turned the track into an instrumental, things perked up. A very sparse sound for its time, showing how Perry was always one step ahead, and issued on a very collectable label."

23. 'Hurry Come Up' - The Crashers (Amalgamated AMG 834) 1969 "A nice Joe Gibbs' Jamaican production sounding very much like The Ethiopians' hit 'Everything Crash'. Some believe it is them in disguise, though the distinctive voice of their leader Leonard Dillon isn't really in evidence."

22. 'Skinheads Don't Fear' - The Hot Rod All Stars (Torpedo TOR 5) 1970 "A clattering breakneck UK instrumental complemented by a one-finger organ made for a non-seller in 1970. If the song didn't have the magic word "skinhead" in the title, this 45 would still be knocking around in the bargain bins in large quantity, as it was in the 80s."

21. 'Deportation' - Monty Morris (Big Shot BI5 13) 1969 "A sweet up-tempo rhythm with Monty singing of the problems of deportation. An unusual 45 due to the lyrics - which on most skinhead reggae records are pretty much just "jump and dance" rather than social comment."

20. 'Kick Me or I'll Kick You' - Cimarrons (Hot Rod HR 105) 1970 "Another UK bovver-boy tune from the Cima-Rods. The attempted rhythm is a JA skin standard known as 'Shocks of Mighty' after the best-known record which uses it, and there's some chatting over the top. It's hidden away on the flipside of a frightful instrumental of the cheesy 'Grandfather's Clock', which tells you a lot about the faith Trojan had in this gem!"

19. 'Tea House from Emperor Roscoe' - Dice the Boss (Joe JRS 3) 1970 "DJ (talking) version of The Openings' 'Tea House', (No 11 below) with Dice carrying the swing over an already great tune."

18. 'Skinheads A Message To You' - Desmond Riley (Down Town DT 450) 1969 "More UK business. Desmond tells the skins to cool it and, for some bizarre reason, draws analogies with John the Baptist. I spoke to the producer, Dandy, about this tune and he admitted he had little idea what Desmond was on about either!"

17. 'Don't Let Me Down' - Marcia Griffiths (Escort ES 808) 1969 "A fast and furious Jamaican cover of a Beatles' classic, beautifully sung and with great rhythm too."

16. 'Splash Down' - The Crystalites (Nu Beat NB 036) 1969 "Jamaican producer Derrick Harriott re-treads the rhythm he used on 'Sufferer', transforming it into a killer instrumental. Very popular at the time and it used to be easy to track down until a few years ago when collectors cottoned on to it. As it's a version of a vocal gem, it's a must-have."

15. 'Skinhead Invasion' - Laurel Aitken (Nu Beat NB 048) 1970 "Aka Apollo 12, this is Laurel again aiming directly at his core audience."

14. 'Skinhead Revolt' - Joe the Boss (Joe JRS9) 1970 "Producer Joe threw everything into this 45: a crunching Rudies' rhythm, chirpy DJ Dice the Boss, and a lazy Rico trombone weaving through the track. Joe also pops up shouting on the title on what is arguably the best made-for-skinheads tune."

13. 'Babam Bam' - The Ravers (Upsetter US 312) 1969 "Lee Perry at his best on this flipside gem, which is a vocal cut to the much-loved 'Live Injection'. The A-side is a heavily-disguised version of The Meters' 'Sophisticated Cissy', here retitled 'Medical Operation', which is also a pretty nifty tune."

12. Skinhead Train - The Charmers (Explosion EX 2045) 1971 "Jamaican producer Lloyd Charmers chugs out a passable chuffing rhythm and delivers plenty of skinhead mentions to keep the collectors happy."

11. 'Tea House' - The Opening (Reggae REG 3001) 1970 "Produced by Joe Mansano, this is actually the premier UK

band, The Rudies, laying down a driving, moody organ instrumental."

10. 'Moonhop in London/Skinhead Moondust' - The Hot Rod All Stars (Torpedo TOR 10) 1970"'Moonhop in London' utilises the bassline of Derrick Morgan's hit 'Moon Hop', which was also borrowed by Symarip on 'Skinhead Moonstomp'. Plenty of references to skinheads and some squeaky organ make for a highly collectable 45."

9. 'Skinhead Speaks His Mind' - The Hot Rod All Stars (Hot Rod HR 104) 1970 "Judging by the paucity of lyrics, this skinhead had little on his mind to speak of! A particularly dreadful UK cash-in record which utilises The Winstons' 'Amen Brother' melody in parts, with a chant of "skinhead, skinhead" tiresomely repeated throughout, amid shouts and grunts."

8. 'Reggae Fever' - Sidney, George & Jackie (AKA the Pioneers) (Attack ATT 8064) 1974 "Bizarre is the best way to describe this record, released some three years after the skins had turned to smooths and disappeared. It's the B-side to a limp chart hopeful, 'At the Club', and is based on The Valentines' rocksteady classic 'Blam Blam Fever'. The guys sing of braces and skinheads to a very ordinary British beat, yet, due to the use of skinhead imagery in the paltry lyrics, it's gained desirable status many years after dying a death in the cut-out bins."

7. 'Dip It Up' - The Sparkers (Black Cat BS 155) 1969 "A top-flight Jamaican jumpy reggae vocal using the rhythm (backing track) also utilised on the great instrumental 'Code It' from Ranford Williams. Actually called 'Dig It Up' but, like many records that originated in Jamaica, something got lost via the transatlantic phone cable."

6. 'V Rocket' - The Fabions (Bullet BU 410) 1969 "This is more like it! A powerhouse Jamaican rhythm, first used by The Tennors on 'Another Scorcher', with some sweet call-and-response and a lead voice praising the V Rocket sound system. Worth every penny!"

5. 'Skinheads A Bash Them' - Claudette (Grape GR 3020) 1970 "Another made-for-skinheads UK recording which comments on the violence that alerted the tabloids to the youth cult. Rhythm-wise it's nothing special, and Claudette isn't a singer with the talent of, say, rocksteady star Phyllis Dillon, but it's now a high flyer price-wise."

4. 'Hold Down' - The Kingstonians (Crab, CRAB 19) 1969 "The skins loved it then and they love it now. Jackie Bernard and his two sidekicks lay down a skinhead staple with great vocals and a rhythm guaranteed to get the tassels tapping."

3. 'Su Su Su' - Soul Directions (Attack ATT 8011) 1969 "Actually a vocal group, The Pioneers, on a rare outing with Jamaican producer Byron Lee. Sweet singing over a nice snappy rhythm."

2. 'Skinheads Are Wrecking the Town' - Laurel Aitken (Ackee ACK 105) 1969 "A highly desirable UK-recorded 45, due to the magic word "skinhead" in the title and the whole song (which is a vague reworking of Desmond Dekker's '007' slowed right down) making constant reference to the bovver-boys. A made-for-skinhead's 45 which, judging by its scarcity and white-label-only release, was not deemed saleable enough to gain a regular issue."

1. 'Black Panther' - Sir Collins & the Black Diamonds (Duke DU 46) 1969 "Clancy Collins specialised in using Jamaican rhythm tracks and overdubbing in London for release on his 1967 Collins' Down Beat label. This powerhouse 45 from a couple of years later also has a very Jamaican feel to the heavyweight rhythm, with the shouted exclamations of Sir Collins referring to the US Black Power movement of the time. An undiscovered gem until it appeared on the Trojan CD *Dancehall 69*; now it's now the most sought-after 45 on this scene."

The End of the Skinhead

"Alas, amazingly the skinhead fashion scene was very brief for most of us, only lasting a year. Our friends down South led the way in growing their hair. Suedeheads and then smooths rapidly gave way to brightly patterned shirts, flares and the beginning of a fashion disaster period! The sight of football fans scrapping in platform shoes, tank tops, flares, etc., was surreal! There were pockets of skinheads in rural UK which had the fashion lingering on but, in the main, by 1970 it was gone for us."

After just a few years, the Skinhead scene began to fade from culture; some left the scene altogether, while others moved into different categories which stemmed from the skinhead cult as it evolved, which included suedeheads (a name stemmed from the growing out of the crop which takes on a suede appearance), smoothies, and bootboys.

In 1971 an article was produced in which three former skinheads, each of whom had belonged to the 'Woolwich Chops', reflected on their time in the culture. John Hainsby, who was 19 at the time, explained:

"It was a laugh. A couple of the happiest years of my life. All the skinheads round here have got married, gone away or been put away now. We've grown up and matured. Like we stopped being skinheads after we had our last kicking.

"It was great then you know. Like everything had a name. When you went out at night, you went out in your Ben Sherman shirt, your Levis and your Doc Martens or your squires. And even when we went down Margate of a weekend you could tell our chaps. We all looked the same, like a uniform in sheepskins, white jeans and boots. We were really together, really good.

"We go to different clubs now and we don't go looking for bother anymore. Like in the old days we always had to have it go off with the Lewisham Mods down Catford, but we don't go where they are now. Mind you, we got very bad. We had some stabbings in Woolwich...murders like. We don't bother with rival gangs anymore. Mind you, if the greasers get a bit lippy down the Starlight club then there's trouble.

"At one time, Woolwich chops used to fight with the Army Squaddies every day and night. They couldn't stand them cos they were right yetis. They thought they owned the place. Now if they see you with long hair, they think you're queer. You can't win. If you had short hair, it labelled you right away with coppers and everyone. You can get a more elegant bird. Like French birds and that. Before, with short hair, they didn't want to know."

Suedeheads, although largely akin to skinheads, would actually grow their hair considerably longer and dressed in a more formal fashion. They wore brogues, loafers or basket weave Norwegians instead of the heavy boot associated with skinheads, Sta-prest trousers in all their various colours, check button-down shirts (Ben Sherman, Jaytex and Brutus were the most popular) and sharp suits as every day wear. These suits were often in Prince of Wales checks or dogtooth patterns, three buttons, narrow shouldered, high buttoning with lapels and waisted as well as Crombie-style overcoats and sheepskin coats. Like the skinheads, suedeheads favoured reggae, ska, and rocksteady, though some also listened to British glam rock.

The girls would often wear boys' shoes, usually loafers, crepe soled lace-ups and other popular high street fashions of the day such as sling-backs with flared heels, suede and patent-leather, buckled shoes which bore bright multicolours towards the end. Mini-skirts worn with geometric patterns, plain and side patterns were popular with the girls, while they would wear the same shirts as the boys, off-the-peg jackets which would be of varying length, although 3/4 length just above the knee was often favoured in 2-tone fabrics, PoW checks, double breasted also. The hair would be slightly longer than the boys, usually in a neat style, parted to display much of the forehead, with the lengths razor cut, sometimes lacquered for effect.

Suedeheads were largely a product of the big cities and towns and were streets ahead in the style game. Although a minority of skinheads had always dressed in what was later seen as the suedehead way, it wasn't really until around 1969 that they began to take on a cult identity of their own. Some suedeheads would embody the look of a city gentleman, carrying an umbrella and wearing a bowler hat. Now, as pretentious as this may all sound, not all were for show. Many boasted highly sharpened metal points which proved useful when it came to fighting. Not only that, but it came in handy for keeping your Crombie coat dry should it rain (many can attest to how repugnant the smell of a soaking wet Crombie is). In fact, for a while there was even a sub-culture known as Crombie boys, who wore similar gear to both skinheads and suedeheads, but their hair would be shoulder length. Even white reggae star Judge Dread bore long, flowing locks as he sang about skinheads, as did much of his audience who were skinheads in almost every way bar the crop. Here's an article that was published in a *Sunday Times* magazine in March 1971:

'The kids call these overcoats Crombies, but they are rarely the genuine article made from the celebrated Crombie cloth. Still, there is a touch of real class tucked into the top pocket – a pure silk handkerchief. This gentlemanly fad started in London, swaggering out from the East End on to the football terraces where it was caught like measles and spread to places as far apart as Highgate and Barnes. Now you can see Crombie boys getting off the football specials from the Midlands and North. It's a look for boys (and a few girls)

between 12 and 20 who want to give themselves a group identity that swings away from the aggressive look of skinheads and rockers; some South London Crombie boys have even been seen with rolled umbrellas. Shoes must be black and clumpy, shirts thinly striped and open necked, trousers knife-creased. When the 'Crombies' are shed as the weather gets warmer, the word is that the ceremonial order will be two-tone mohair suits – one of the gents in the chair has already been for a fitting. Shirts will have unbuttoned down collars. Black and white patents will probably be the shoe.'

Yet later in 1971 many suedeheads were letting their hair grow and had moved on to becoming smoothies, while others still embraced a mixture of skinhead, suedehead, smoothie and boot boy styles. Smoothies took the name from the style of the hair, which was short on top and collar length at the back and sides. They were also called this because of their preference for plain shoes which weren't capped or studded. In comparison to their suedehead counterparts, they dressed far more casually, usually wearing round collared shirts, cords, Rupert the Bear check trousers, jumpers and sleeveless jumpers named tank tops which came in a range of different colours. Yet, when it came to going out and about at night, the traditional tonic suits and Crombies were still worn.

To many people, smoothies appeared as very ordinary with no distinct uniform to distinguish their identity. Even though most smoothies had been skinheads just a few years before, all links to the skin culture had all but gone. The cult didn't last too long and never scaled the heights of popularity as either the skinheads or suedeheads and it all but vanished within a considerably short time.

However, one cult that lasted far longer than smoothies was the bootboy cult. Bootboys were a more natural progression from skinhead for many. Yet, whereas skinheads and suedes were mainly about the music and fashion, these aspects played a secondary role for this particular subculture; it was more about gang life than anything else. It also signalled a return back to what skinheads termed aggro, fights over territory, be it a town, village, a football end or pub at stake. While ska, reggae and soul were still highly popular with some bootboys, others would prefer to follow what was on offer in the latest chart.

The cult represented terrace fashion and gangs of bootboys were often referred to as mobs. There were even gangs of bootgirls that formed mobs, making quite a name for themselves in the process. Previously, many bootboys and girls had been skinheads, although some had missed out on the suedehead and smoothie phases. Most were in their late teens and early twenties and some saw themselves as being superior to skinheads. In fact, any skinhead firms that were still about by this time were written off as "backward has-beens". The word on the street was that should the skinheads be looking for action (in other words, fighting) in a nearby town, they would get all tooled up and travel there by bus. The bootboys, however, would usually organise a series of cars and vans to transport them there and back in style.

Football was predominantly the highlight of every bootboy's week. They would wear white butchers coats which would usually bear the team's name stencilled on the back and blood splattered over it for added effect. This represented the height of terrace style at this point in time. While legend has it that Chelsea's Shed started the craze, it had soon widely spread to many in attendance at football grounds all over England. Not only that, but there were a minority of gangs that would turn up dressed in white boiler suits, inspired by the film *A Clockwork Orange*, which had struck a chord with many skinheads and bootboys. Football violence prevailed and, typically, the media hyped this up in their stories. At football grounds you could guarantee there would be television news cameras there, waiting and hoping for some action to capture on film. Every Saturday evening on the news there would always be pictures of fans climbing on the roofs of stands to throw things at the police.

Interestingly, a skinhead turned journalist by the name of Chris Lightbrown produced a guide to football grounds in 1972 for *The Sunday Times*. In this piece he also cited the top names in the world of football aggro, and coming up highest were Manchester United, Manchester City, West Ham, Spurs and Stoke City. He also went on to point out that the real reason for dwindling attendances at football matches wasn't a result of football hooliganism, but rather more because of the standard of play.

Aside from the boots and the aggro, the terrace bootboys had very little in common with the skinheads who had previously reigned. By 1972, there were very few traces of the skinhead style left and if there were, it was mainly confined to northern outposts, the cult surviving there as late as 1974. Even though the cult never died out completely, it was really now left to the individuals to fly the flag as opposed to fully-fledged mobs and crews.

The Revival of the Skinhead

"We were a result of social conditions at the time. We were unconscious youths looking for direction. Perfect demonization fodder. And you know we were fucking angry as well, the bottom line being, if you're gonna go down on somebody, they're either gonna go down on their knees or fight back! The ones that were abused, the ones that were broken, they found their tribe together. They could protect each other. And all of that with unconscious understanding of your energy and who you are." -Gavin Watson, Wycombe Skin

"Skinheads appear to favour disorder. They are lords of misrule. Many seem not to have progressed much beyond the desire to break up society, without much desire to restructure it." --Jack B. Moore

"Remember seeing Skinheads in the Essex town that I grew up in and them scaring the shit out of me just by their presence. I eventually got into the Scooter scene in the early 80's and there were loads but mainly all good-natured and lovers of reggae. A minority were racist and just wanted to confront anyone who looked at them the wrong way."

"The Union Jack became a very, very important symbol for us. We were English, we were working-class, and we were very, very proud of that. And the Government at the time was trying to tell us 'no you're not'. We were the abused kids of that time and we were violent as fuck, 'cos all we knew was violence. We were getting caned by the fucking school teachers. We were getting beaten up by the police. And we were getting double beaten up by our parents, our fathers. I mean, my dad was a drunk who

would whack us round with leather straps. And that was normal. It wasn't anything unusual: it's just how it was. It was just part of our culture. Loads of the girls were sexually abused. Loads of them. Of course these kids are gonna react to that. They're gonna be violent. They're gonna take out their anger any way they can. But we were an army...a community of children on council estates that were just completely abused by everybody. We took on society with our weapons being boots, braces and our mates. We actually were no major threat, but people thought we were."
    -- Symond Lawes, Wycombe Skin

"Betrayed? Yeah, course I feel betrayed. It's like everything's gone back to what it was like in '74 and '75. But I honestly think it's started again in the East End. The feeling's coming back again." --Micky Geggus, Cockney Rejects, 1979

After the emergence of punk rock, a form of rock music that developed between 1974 and 1976 in the US, UK and Australia, the skinhead culture was revived in the late 1970s. Punk was spearheaded by the likes of Iggy Pop and the Sex Pistols. Punks were more concerned with visual than physical confrontation. This style was more about anarchy and chaos, attacking the establishment with words and images, masking the actual violence of their lifestyles. Many punks took to adopting swastikas more in an effort to shock than with any real desire to support the right-wing organisations. Such fascist and racist images ensured their notoriety and the rejection by much of their older generation.

The appropriation of the paraphernalia of threat and violence was reflected in the performance style of the likes of Sid Vicious, who would often smash glass and deliberately cut themselves during performances, heightening the dark image they intentionally conveyed. This so-called bravado of self-mutilation was further enhanced by the many multiple piercings of several punks. The style was considerably self-absorbed, parading its many self-inflicted wounds in front of a society they perceived as rather bland and very uncaring, while threatening the destruction of this society with extreme cut-up graphics, and blatant antagonistic musical styles.

Many of these revivalist skinheads responded to the widespread commercial impact of punk by adopting the look that was in line with the original skinheads. While the skinhead style never totally died out in the East End or in the Midlands, very few skins could be spotted on the streets between 1972 and 1976. In the ensuing years, the growing punk subculture saw them often fighting with the Teds in the King's Road, Chelsea, usually on a Saturday afternoons. Each of these opposing groups had their own group of skinhead supporters, many of whom were part of a skinhead revival. Those part of the skinhead revival would often side with the teds, who were mainly pro-British and all for the Union Jack. In contrast to this were the punks who were anti-royalist and thought nothing of sticking safety-pins into pictures of the Queen. The skins who tended to side with the punks were a new breed, all of whom wished to be viewed as more anarchical and even more shocking than the punks.

How the new skins achieved this was by reviving the more extreme elements of the traditional skinhead look and vastly exaggerating them. Their heads would be shaved completely, or the crop would be bleached, some with Union Jacks or other symbols dyed into it. Mohicans were

particularly popular among some and it was really only the
boots, jeans and braces that were a nod to the original style.
The swastika adorned many a punk T-shirt and was flaunted
by many in the form of facial tattoos, while they would taunt
the public with Nazi salutes. The skins conveyed the image
of a robotic-like uniformed army, in which to attack just one
individual would provoke a severely violent response from
the rest.

On the subject of racism, one skinhead told author Nick
Knight in *Skinhead*: "The Spades have got their own culture.
Don't get me wrong. I've got a lot of coloured friends. And
they're decent people. But they've got their own culture. The
Pakistanis have a culture. It's thousands of years old. But
where's our culture? Where's the British culture? You wear
the flag and everybody slags you off for being a Nazi. But
it's got nothing to do with being a Nazi as far as I'm
concerned...We fought the Germans, the London

people...They (the skinheads) are just wearing the flag because they're patriotic. What's wrong with being patriotic? This is England. And they don't live here. They know nothing about it. They're living in detached houses. Driving around in a Rolls. Be honest. What the fuck are they going to know about us...?"

Another skinhead at the time also told the same author: "A Rasta can wear a Black is Beautiful badge and they all sit up and start clapping. I wear a White is Beautiful badge and get run in for being racist...All skins are for the flag but that doesn't mean they're all NF or British movement. Some are but most aren't. It's like any other group...How can I put it? You went to college so you got into the Socialist Worker's Party or whatever. Naturally. For people like me it's natural to be patriotic and to stick with your mates..."

One skinhead readily admitted to Nick Knight that he joined the British Movement and his reasons for doing so: "For the crack, like. But they went on about Hitler. He's dead. I couldn't see the point..."

The skins who supported the teds were very much traditionalists. They were akin to what the original skins had been, with their sharp and smart dress sense, working-class ethics and attitudes. These skins actually regarded the punks in the same light as the originals had with the middle class hippies in the late 1960s. They totally detested these new plastic skins. There were many pubs in London which were often predominantly made up of the original skinheads, most of whom tended to be above the age of 25, and at which none of these new boots (which were often knee-high), braces and plastic skins would be tolerated.

Somewhere between these two factions were the emergence of Madness and a wave of 2-Tone bands. Madness was all about fun and dancing and their music embodied old ska and rocksteady styles. "*Fuck Art - let's dance*" was their well-known motto, but also reflected the feelings of most of these new dance bands.

In the beginning of their career, Madness gained a huge skinhead following, but, unfortunately, the music press would highlight the fact that some of the new skins that were fans were also members of far-right political groups such as the British Movement, leading to them (unfairly) declaring Madness a 'fascist band'.

Photographer Gavin Watson once recalled about this period: "I grew up on a council estate in High Wycombe, Buckinghamshire, around gangs and with no real education. It's strange looking back. My elder brother was a big reggae fan and I grew up listening to the music. Before Madness was on TV I hadn't even heard of a skinhead, I didn't even know they existed. Perhaps I was just cut off from culture. But ska and reggae music hit us in a different way – I was opened up to a culture that I never knew existed. My brother got so into it. I was more 'combat trousers and ready for aggro', but my brother would invest time tracking down obscure records. Of course there was no internet back then so getting hold of the music was all part of it. The punk element came along and next minute I know I'm an uneducated angry young man."

Originally called The North London Invaders when they formed in 1976, Madness first comprised of members Mike Barson on keyboards and vocals, Chris Foreman on guitar and Lee Thompson on saxophone and vocals. Later on, they recruited John Hasler on drums and Chas Smash on bass guitar, before being joined by lead vocalist Dikron Tulane. The following year, Suggs (Graham McPherson) replaced Tulane as lead singer of the group and Smash departed to be replaced by Gavin Rodgers. Drummer Daniel Woodgate and bass player Mark Bedford would join the group in 1978. After switching their name to Morris and the Minors for a brief period, they finally altered their name permanently to Madness, named after one of their favourite songs by legendary ska/reggae artist, Prince Buster.

Mike Barson was said to be somewhat displeased with the group's association with the skinhead subculture, most likely owing to the press branding them fascists. Before becoming a full-time member of Madness, Chas Smash had even become involved in fights with some skinheads at performances. During one performance in 1979, where the group were supported by Red Beans and Rice, who featured a black lead singer, the band found themselves unable to complete their performance thanks to constant racist chants from certain members of the largely skinhead audience. Despite Suggs later coming back out on stage to declare his disgust at this racist behaviour, this still failed to stop some of the audience Nazi saluting.

In an article in *NME* magazine in 1979, speculation was fuelled further about the band being a racist band supporting the National Front, when he was quoted as saying, 'We don't care if people are in the NF as long as they're having a good time.' This statement was something the rest of the band were keen to distance themselves from and, likewise, it was certainly something the press didn't want to hear either. Yet as politically incorrect this may have sounded, he may have had a point, as how were the group to know who and who weren't supporters of the NF unless it was tattooed across their forehead? To some of the kids at the time, it seemed fashionable to them to be labelled as NF supporters as it was an act of rebellion and a deliberate attempt to cause a stir. Some of these young skinheads were not even remotely interested in politics.

At this point in time, a lot of the kids called themselves rude boys or rude girls. These were mainly white kids and whose love of the music stretched no further than their love for 2-Tone related bands, such as Madness and The Specials. Black and white was the strict dress code.

Coventry-based band The Specials (also known as The Special AKA) had been a support act for The Clash during their *On Parole* tour in 1978. First formed in 1977, the band hadn't gone down well with the crowd during this tour, the skinheads just simply not taking to their fusion of punk and reggae.

After the tour had finished, the group retreated to Coventry and back to playing the back rooms of pubs. Founded by songwriter and keyboardist Jerry Dammers, vocalist Tim Strickland, guitarist/vocalist Lynval Golding, drummer Silverton Hutchinson and bassist Horace Panter, Strickland was eventually replaced by Terry Hall. Like Madness, the group had undergone a number of name changes, first being called the Automatics before switching to the Coventry Automatics. Upon vocalist Neville Staple and guitarist Roddy Byers joining the band in 1978, they then altered their name to The Special AKA.

The Specials began at the same time as Rock against Racism, a campaign set up in the UK in 1976 as a direct response to the increase in racial conflict and growth of white nationalist groups such as the NF. The Race Relations Act of 1965 had been extended in 1968, seeking to assert more rights and equality for ethnic minorities, which antagonised right-wing white people. Many pop, rock, punk and reggae artists staged concerts with an anti-racist theme, urging young people against racism.

By 1979, following the departure of Silverton Hutchinson who was replaced by John Bradbury, Jerry Dammers formed the 2-Tone Records label and released the group's debut single 'Gangsters', a reworking of Prince Busters' classic 'Al Capone'. The 2-Tone label boasted several acts that all entwined ska and reggae elements with pop and punk overtones. It bore a distinctive sound, just as labels such as

Motown and Stax had back in the sixties with their brand of soul. Among the other signings to the label were the likes of Bad Manners (*Dance Craze* only), The Beat (known as The English Beat in the States), Madness, Rico Rodriguez, Rhoda Dakar, The Bodysnatchers, and The Selecter.

Back in 1978, a gig in Bracknell had been disrupted by neo-Nazi skinheads who were there in support of the street punk band Sham 69. The National Front had by now instigated a programme of "direct action", which infiltrated football hooligans and skinheads: "bovver" at concerts was suddenly the far-right's new route to gain attention from the media. That same year, seig heiling skinheads had caused over £7,500 worth of damage during a Sham 69 concert held at the London School of Economics. Jerry Dammers of The Specials recalled in an interview for *The Guardian* many years later:

"In Bracknell, the Sham Army turned up, got onstage and attacked the lead singer of Suicide, the other support band. That was the night the Specials concept was born. I idealistically thought, 'we have to get through to these people'. It was obvious that a mod and skinhead revival was coming, and I was trying to find a way to make sure it didn't go the way of the National Front and the British Movement. I saw punk as a piss-take of rock music, as rock music committing suicide, and it was great and it was really funny, but I couldn't believe people took it as a serious musical genre which they then had to copy. It seemed to be a bit healthier to have an integrated kind of British music, rather than white people playing rock and black people playing their music. Ska was an integration of the two."

The Specials adopted the sixties look of the Jamaican rude boys, intertwined with a few other styles that Dammers had picked up from his days as a mini-mod and suedehead. These included pork pie hats, wraparound shades, mohair suits, button down shirts, white socks and black loafers, in turn bringing the famous 2-Tone logo, Walt Jabsco, to life.

While certain punk bands like Sham had helped in reviving the skinhead faithful, it was really 2-Tone that provided the skinhead scene with a more authentic soundtrack to dance to. Through their many support slots with various punk bands, The Specials had gained a wide skinhead audience. In April 1979, they scored one of their first big London dates when they supported The Damned and The U.K. Subs. The latter group had amassed quite a significant skinhead following themselves and they were instantly impressed with The Specials magical brand of ska. These same skinheads soon frequented Specials' gigs from there on in.

The Specials certainly weren't the only bands embracing ska and reggae sounds: There were bands like UB40 and The Beat, both from Birmingham, doing similar kinds of things, while London had groups like Madness and Bad Manners, who were both beginning to make their mark. After The Specials' success with their 'Gangsters' single, they no longer found themselves confined to support acts for numerous punk acts. They had created the biggest waves in the industry since the Sex Pistols and had no problem filling out any venue they played at.

In late July 1979, a 2-Tone night was staged at Camden Town's Electric Ballroom, which saw the likes of The Specials, Madness and The Selecter bringing crowds of skinheads, mods and punks in. Madness were well on their way to having the biggest skinhead following at this stage. As fate would have it, lead singer Suggs met up with The Specials at the Hope & Anchor one night and not before long the two groups were sharing the bill with one another.

Likewise, Bad Manners had, too, amassed a huge skinhead following, a group led by Doug Trendle who was better known as Buster Bloodvessel. His trademark was boasting a 13-inch tongue and his completely bald head. He would jump about on stage in his boots and jeans, heavily sweating and singing about skinheads, booze and fat people. While Madness had delivered their debut single, 'The Prince', via the 2-Tone label, Bad Manners went down a different path and signed to the Magnet label. This still didn't prevent them from pumping out hits with stompers like 'Special Brew' and 'Lip Up Fatty'.

The likes of The Specials and Madness had certainly attracted a new generation of skinheads into the fold, many of whom weren't the slightest bit interested in punk music. They loved this new breed of ska music and skinhead reggae, both of which was quickly revived in the clubs and at concerts.

While much of this music united many skinheads, there were still many incidents where outbreaks of violence escalated over football, politics or allegiance to a cult. Some would turn up at gigs waiting and hoping for it all to kick off. The 50-date 2-Tone tour saw numerous violent incidents throughout its run, none more so than at Hatfield Poly just a week into its tour. Midway through The Selecters' performance, a gang of over 30 had broken their way into a bar area through a fire exit, and began attacking people with Stanley knives and razors. These same people - all men - had been refused entry earlier as they had been parading banners around declaring themselves "The Hatfield Mafia" and "Hatfield Anti-Fascist League", and were obviously hunting down National Front supporters. None of this gang stopped to talk about political affiliations and they assumed anyone that bore a crop and wearing boots were automatically aligned with the NF. By the end of the night, ten people were hospitalised, eleven were arrested and over a thousand pounds worth of damage had been done to the building.

Many skinheads who were lovers of all things 2-Tone were not in support of either the NF or the equally notorious British Movement. Yet despite the multi-racial nature of the 2-Tone bands, some sections of these crowds were vocal in their support to the extreme right. Ironic. The tabloids caught on to this and immediately began associating all 2-Tone bands with some sort of musical fascist movement. The Rock against Racism movement even took to having the odd dig at such ska bands, accusing them of not doing enough to eradicate racism, an unfair accusation to say the least. Neville Staple of The Specials recalled: "At the time it was 'no Blacks, no Pakis, and no Irish'. It was the National Front against us - black and white joining and being on stage together. We used to get a lot of conflict at our gigs."

Madness found themselves at the heart of such criticism, particularly as all members of the group were white. The nutty boys, as they were known by fans, made it clear that they were not interested in politics, were totally against racism and totally opposed to the NF. Did the media listen? In some aspects, evidently not. Suggs, the lead singer, commented at the time, "There's no way we're political. We're certainly not fucking fascists. If we were fascists, what would we be doing playing ska and bluebeat? If we'd wanted to talk about politics we'd have formed a debating society, not a fucking band." They even told their fans that should the violence at their gigs not stop the band would not only stop playing, but also all go their own separate ways. It still didn't stop many NF skins turning up at their concerts though. Soon, the group were of the mind-set that they could perhaps reach out to their fans who were NF supporters, and try and convert them. Similarly, The Beat and The Specials took this stance too. And in some cases this worked and some were actually educated and reformed, some leaving concerts without the NF badge they had arrived with.

It was an awkward predicament to be in, as none of the bands wanted to turn their backs on their skinhead followings but at the same time they didn't want the violence at their gigs. These bands acknowledged that it was the skinheads that helped the bands on their roads to success. When many clubs started introducing a policy of no skinheads allowed, acts like the Bodysnatchers and The Specials refused to play at them.

A journalist recalled a violent encounter at a gig he'd fallen victim to: 'I remember going to a Secret Affair show at the Rainbow. I was going as a reviewer so I wasn't part of that tribe that had gone - they were the post-Paul Weller mods. I left early and was slashed by a gang of skinheads with a Stanley knife who assumed I was a mod. Rather futilely as I fell to the floor with my lip bleeding I said, 'I'm not a mod, I'm post-punk!''

Much of the violence at 2-Tone gigs was often aimed at the non-ska support bands. For example, the skinheads refused to let Echo & the Bunnymen complete their set when they were playing on the same bill as Madness and Bad Manners at the Electric Ballroom. Red Beans & Rice suffered the same fate when Madness returned to the Ballroom a few months later, while Holly and The Italians were forced to quit their support slot on The Selecter's 2 Tone tour after many of their fans had been attacked at their gigs.

It must be noted, though, that many concerts went off without a single bit of trouble, many mods and skinheads uniting to simply just enjoy an evening's entertainment watching their favourite bands (although there were always several police vans parked down side streets when it came to finishing time, all waiting for it to just all kick off). In fact, skins and mods were often united when it came to Bank Holiday rucks with teds and rockers, and trouble ran rife in the likes of Brighton, Scarborough, Great Yarmouth and Rhyl, all of which often made the evening news headlines.

Mod versus skin battles didn't really occur until 2- Tone started to give way to Oi!, though that's not how the media saw it, who claimed everyone and everything was a potential target for a spot of skinhead aggro. Mixed armies of mods, skinheads and rudies became a common sight, as they waged war against their enemies, just as had been the case in the sixties. In April 1980, trouble at Southend during a Bank Holiday weekend made the front of many tabloid covers. An accompanying article in the *Daily Star*, titled 'Mods and Wreckers', read:

'THE BOOT went in all around Britain yesterday as skinheads, mods and rockers went on a seaside rampage. Ugly scenes like this sent holidaymakers scattering in terror at a string of resorts.

'At Southend, over 1,000 skinheads ran amok after foiling a police plan to run them out of town. They were herded on to two special trains back to London - but jumped off just outside the resort after the train drivers refused to carry on.

'Within an hour hundreds were marauding along the seafront again, spreading violence and terror. Two press photographers were beaten up and thrown in the sea - one losing a camera worth £2000.'

Not all photographers were treated with such hostility, as renowned photographer Derek Ridgers can attest to. Ridgers photographed many skinheads between the summer of 1979 and the summer of 1984, either in London or in seaside towns where much of the violence ensued during Bank Holiday weekends. In fact, many of his skinhead photo collections would appear in a show called *Skinheads* at the Chenil Studio

Gallery in Chelsea, October 1980. Contrary to the speculative view of the media, Ridgers' memories of the skinheads are certainly far from bad as he recalled in a media interview several years later:

"In early '79 I was already engaged in what eventually turned out to be a lengthy photographic study of New Romantics (though back then they were not known as such).

"I'd been documenting this nascent scene in the Soho nightclub 'Billy's' and, one evening, a group of about half-a-dozen skinheads turned up. They saw me taking photographs and one of them, a guy called Wally, asked me if I'd like to take some photos of them too. They seemed pretty friendly and not at all camera shy. I took a few snaps, we got talking and Wally suggested I go with the whole gang on one of their Bank Holiday jaunts to the seaside.

"That was what led, eventually, to five years of photographing skinheads. In those five years I got to know some of the skinheads quite well and liked many of them. Almost all were polite and courteous to me. I saw virtually no violence, just a handful of scuffles. If I had seen any fighting, I certainly wouldn't have photographed it for the simple reason that I wouldn't have wanted the presence of me and my camera to affect the situation."

David Rumsey, who ran the publication *Tighten Up Skinzine* from 1989 - 1996, recalled about Bank Holiday aggro:

'One of the most important aspects of being a skin when I first embraced the cult was Bank Holiday Mondays. A day where I would escape the mundane life that I led, and join hundreds of others for a few hours of merriment.

'I didn't walk to the seafront. I swaggered. I felt like I could take on the whole world. And when I saw the first group of skins, my heart would fill with pride. I was part of an army and for a day the town would be ours.

'The police, in their infinite wisdom, would confiscate our laces and braces in a vain attempt to curb the violence. I didn't care, my jeans were skin tight and a pocket full of paper clips soon solved the lace problem.

'Putting on Cockney accents, my mates and I would spin a web of lies to the best looking girls we could find. With a bit of luck I'd end up with a quick fondle and a love bite on my neck, which I could show off to my school mates, telling them ever wilder stories about how I got it.

'The hardest part for me was how to obtain beer. Being only a young pup of 15, shopkeepers always asked my age. When I told them I was 18, they would laughingly send me on my way empty handed. Never mind. There was always an obliging older skin who would get some for me for the price of a can. And with a four pack under my arm, I felt a mile high.

'Later, when the pubs had kicked out their drunken contents, all the skins would meet up. It was time for some heads to be bashed, and more often than not, one of them was mine.

'The police would view us as the enemy. Any chance they got, they would give you hassle. They would move us on to the beach, make us empty out our pockets and ask stupid questions like, "What are you doing in Margate son?" I would have thought the answer was obvious. We were after some aggro, but the usual answer was, "Just having a laugh."

'As the afternoon wore on, the Old Bill would form snatch squads, and a few of us would be carted off to the local cop shop. This was the place to exchange stories of birds we'd had and fights we'd won.

'After a couple of hours, the police would let us go, usually without any charges, and we would amble off home. The next day at school, sporting a black eye or a thick lip, I would tell my mates all about when the boot went in.

'These were the days when skins were kings, and to mess meant a good kicking.'

The Rise & Fall of 2 Tone

"It is not enough to be anti-racist yourself. You have to be a positive anti-racist. You have to stand against it, because otherwise nothing changes it."
--Jerry Dammers, The Specials

"Everyone puts the skinheads down but they never mention the good side. At Dingwalls, for example, the skins went around stopping all the trouble."
--Chas Smash, Madness

In the early eighties, Madness had made such a name for themselves they went on a tour in the States. Upon their return, the band made a bid to break away from the skinhead tag they had been branded with. The group's sound steadily progressed into more mainstream pop, some skinheads seeing this as a sell-out. However, they still retained their many skinhead fans who still faithfully turned out to their gigs and the nutty boys never stopped including hits in their set like 'One Step Beyond', 'Night Boat to Cairo' and 'My Girl', all of which had helped gain them such a wide skinhead audience in the first place.

As luck would have it, it turned out Madness had made the right move at exactly the right time. After they'd signed to the Stiff label, there began a 2 Tone backlash, starting with The Bodysnatchers during the summer of 1980. Hard to believe it had been just over a year when 'Gangsters' by The Specials had enjoyed top twenty success. Just a few short months earlier, the music press had been showering praise on 2 Tone, but within a flash it was suddenly being deemed as old hat, the critics just waiting for the first flop. On the receiving end of such bashings were Bad Manners, many writing their songs off as nothing more than superficial nonsense. They were also accused of jumping on the bandwagon and attempting to cash in on the success of the likes of Madness, The Selecter and The Specials.

Suddenly, releases by bands such as Mobster and The Ska Dows were being dismissed before even reaching reviewers. The Bodysnatchers were a relatively inexperienced all-female group who had been lucky enough to score a hit single before more established bands had. It was because of this that they started receiving harsh criticism from the media. 'Let's Do Rock Steady' had been a cover version of a Dandy Livingstone classic and the press were soon labelling them as "Two Tone Tessies". Yet bands like The Beat enjoyed hits with cover versions of Smokey Robinson & The Miracles' 'The Tears of A Clown', many had a shot at Prince Buster's 'Madness' and UB40 wound up being highly successful with their *Labour of Love* albums that contained nothing but covers.

On the positive side, though, this brought attention to songs that may well have been forgotten had they not been revived and given a whole new lease of life for a new generation of skinheads. This created a high demand for the originals and record labels like Trojan and Island began digging into their vaults and re-releasing songs like 'Skinhead Moonstomp' by Symarip, which would re-enter the lower reaches of the chart. Not only that, but legends on the ska and reggae scene like Desmond Dekker, Prince Buster and Judge Dread retreated to the recording studios to record new material. Laurel Aitken was even able to notch up his first chart hit with 'Rudi Got Married' (released on the I Spy label), and such artists were suddenly in-demand performers, skinheads delighting in being able to see these performers back on stage.

Throughout 1980, the likes of Jimmy Cliff, Toots & the Maytals, Desmond Dekker, The Heptones, Laurel Aitken and Judge Dread would soon be performing for both the old and new generation of skinheads, and all of these artists acknowledged 2 Tone bands as having revived the classic sounds of Jamaica.

However, The Selecter, having had enough of all the backlash, swiftly exited 2 Tone and signed to Chrysalis. Unfortunately for them, this proved to be their undoing, as apart from a few singles and a second album named *Celebrate the Bullet*, they didn't make it past 1981. A sad end for a group that were, at one point, tipped to be one of the biggest of the eighties.

Likewise, The Specials wanted to break free of their past and adopt a new musical style. This change of direction was signalled by the release of their album *More Specials*. While the album still held vague hints of a ska sound, much of the project heavily captured more soul and rockabilly styles. In the process, the group also abandoned the suits and loafers in favour of a more casual look. Yet The Specials still continued to perform the likes of 'Rat Race', 'A Message to You Rudy' and 'Concrete Jungle' in their gigs, and they still had no problem selling out at venues they performed at.

The main problem at these gigs, all of which were still filled by skinheads, mods, rudies and the odd punk, were the stage invasions during sets. Stage invasions had become something of a tradition with all ska bands, but just as had been the case with Sham, they were becoming increasingly difficult to control. When The Specials would hit the stage, many would jump up on stage to be with the band, and it reached a point where songs were being interrupted simply because the musicians didn't have the space to play in.

In The Specials case, they built higher layers for the band to retreat to, rather than put up barricades. This led to disastrous consequences in the summer of 1980, when during a gig at Skegness, the stage ended up collapsing under the weight of so many on it. A reluctant decision to keep the stage clear at all times during performances resulted in a riot when the band played at the Emerald Isle in Dublin. In a fund-raising gig held at the Starlight Ballroom, much of the audience members ended up fighting with bouncers in a bid to get to the stage at the Starlight Ballroom. Despite lead singer Terry Hall's cries of "No violence! We hate violence!" this did little to defuse the situation. Not long after this, the venue was burnt down, killing forty-eight people in the process and leaving one hundred-and-twenty-eight severely injured.

 Unlike Madness, who had by now adopted more pop styles to their music, The Specials' change of musical direction still didn't stop skinhead aggro at their concerts. Trouble escalated at Cardiff, Newcastle and Edinburgh during their *More Specials* tour. While The Specials would always do their best to calm the crowds down, they also weren't prepared to simply stand by and watch some of the over-zealous bouncers kicking some kid's head in. Following an incident at Cambridge, with over 3,500 fans crammed in to a huge tent on Midsummer Common, trouble had broken out over football. This led to Jerry Dammers and Terry Hall being charged for inciting a riot, both ending up having to pay thousand pound fines.

The Specials had, by now, had more than enough. Each member of the group went on to work on separate projects and their splitting up was inevitable. That was before they were to enjoy their biggest hit single. By the summer of 1981, unemployment had reached an all-time high and many of England's inner cities were going up in flames. The Specials' released the sublime 'Ghost Town', which rapidly became a number one hit. No song was able to so accurately capture the state of the nation as 'Ghost Town'.

Following this legendary classic, The Specials disbanded and 2 Tone was just about finished, even though it soldiered on until 1985. For just two eventful years, the sounds of 2 Tone had filled countless ordinary kids' lives with something meaningful. While the fire of 2 Tone was put out in 1981, Oi! had already replaced it in the skinhead world.

Below is a full UK discography of 2 Tone releases - singles and albums - from 1979 - 1985, plus the compilations that were issued with 2 Tone catalogue numbers.

Singles

Catalogue no Title	Year	Artist
TT1/TT2 Gangsters	1979	The Special AKA vs The Selecter
CHS TT3 The Prince	1979	Madness
CHS TT4 On My Radio	1979	The Selecter
CHS TT5 A Message to You Rudy	1979	The Specials (featuring Rico)
CHS TT6 Tears of a Clown	1979	The Beat
CHS TT7 I Can't Stand Up for Falling Down	1980	Elvis Costello
CHS TT7 Too Much Too Young	1980	The Special AKA
CHS TT8 Three Minute Hero	1980	The Selecter
CHS TT9 Let's Do Rock Steady	1980	The Bodysnatchers
CHS TT10 Missing Words	1980	The Selecter

CHS TT11 Rat Race	1980	The Specials
CHS TT12 Easy Life	1980	The Bodysnatchers
CHS TT13 Stereotype	1980	The Specials
CHS TT14 Mantovani	1980	The Swinging Cats
CHS TT15 Sea Cruise	1980	Rico
CHS TT16 Do Nothing	1980	The Specials
CHS TT17 Ghost Town	1981	The Specials
CHS TT18 The Boiler	1982	Rhoda & The Special AKA
CHS TT19 Jungle Music	1982	Rico & The Special AKA
CHS TT20 The Feeling's Gone	1982	The Appollinaires
CHS TT21 Tear the Whole Thing Down	1982	The Higsons
CHS TT22 Envy the Love	1982	The Appollinaires
CHS TT23 War Crimes	1982	The Special AKA
CHS TT24 Run Me Down	1983	The Higsons
CHS TT25 Racist Friend	1983	The Special AKA
CHS TT26 Nelson Mandela	1984	The Special AKA

CHS TT27 What I Like Most About You Is Your Girlfriend	1984	The Special AKA
CHS TT28 Window Shopping	1985	The Friday Club
CHS TT29 The Alphabet Army	1986	JB's Allstars
CHS TT30 Ghost Town (Revisited)	1991	The Specials/Special Productions
CHS TT31 The 2 Tone EP	1993	Various
CHS TT32 Sock It To 'Em J.B. (DUB)	2014	The Specials

Albums

CDL TT 5001 Specials	1979	The Specials
CDL TT 5002 Too Much Pressure	1980	The Selecter
CHR TT 5003 More Specials	1981	The Specials
CHR TT 5004 Dance Craze	1981	Various
CHR TT 5005 That Man Is Forward	1981	Rico

CHR TT 5006 Jama Rico	1982	Rico
CHR TT 5007 This Are Two Tone	1983	Various
CHR TT 5008 In The Studio	1984	The Special AKA
CHR TT 5009 The 2 Tone Story	1989	Various
CHR TT 5010 The Specials Singles	1991	The Specials
CHR TT 5011 Live at the Moonlight Club	1992	The Specials
CHR TT 5012 The Best of 2 Tone	1993	Various
CHR TT 5013 The Compact 2 Tone Story	1998	Various

Oi!

"The far-right political groups were looking for any kids that were alienated and these kids were putting on the [skinhead] uniform and going to the gigs. The two recruiting grounds were "Oi" music and football violence....It's unfortunate that the racist elements have become such a by-word for skinhead culture. The media has played its part in this, but by the same token it's clear the fascist element has always been fairly vocal in skinhead culture. The sad bit is that the more enlightened, anti-fascist aspects have not better promoted themselves."   --Bill Osgerby

"A strong, vital look with its roots firmly in the sections of working class Britain which EMBRACED immigrants, their culture and their music. This image was sadly hijacked by fascists, but then recently has been turned on its head once again and adopted by homosexuals, the very subject of right wing vilification. It's a look which has over the years represented many sections of the political spectrum. So anyone who believes they can say exactly how every skinhead will behave is simply mistaken. Vive la skinhead!"
      --Jason, London, UK.

"Oi! is rock and roll, beer, sex, going to gigs, havin' a laugh, fighting back, it's our life, it's our show, our world, our way of life."   --Garry Johnson

The Oi! movement was partly a reaction to the widely held perception that many participants in the early punk rock scene were, according to guitarist Steve Kent of The Business, "Trendy University people using long words, trying to be artistic...and losing touch." Andre Schlesinger of the group The Press said, "Oi! shares many similarities with folk music, besides its often simple musical structure; quaint in some respects and crude in others, not to mention brutally honest, it usually tells a story based in truth." An example of this would be 'Such Fun', from *Oi! Oi! That's Yer Lot!* by The Blood, an extension of the Sex Pistols' 1977 song, 'God Save The Queen', a scathing song about those that abuse their power who hold themselves in a royal or religious majesty.

Oi! had really become an acknowledged genre in the latter half of the 1970s, rearing its head after the perceived commercialisation of punk-rock, and prior to the dominating · hard-core punk sound. The style marked a fusion of early punk bands such as the Ramones, The Clash, The Jam, and the Sex Pistols, intertwined with elements of British rock bands from the 1960s such as The Who and Small Faces, football chants, pub rock bands such as Dr. Feelgood, Eddie and the Hot Rods and The 101ers, and various glam rock bands such as Sweet and Slade. It was in 1980 while writing for the UK weekly pop/rock music newspaper *Sounds*, that Gary Bushell labelled the movement Oi!, while first generation Oi! bands like Sham 69 and Cock Sparrer had been around for years before their style of music was described as such. The guitarist with The Last Resort commented, "Oi! started after Sham 69 got famous. All of a sudden, they didn't want to know the skins. And we were the ones who put them up there in the first place. The Sham Army..."

Bushell had taken the name from the rather garbled "Oi!" that Stinky Turner of band Cockney Rejects would use as an introduction to their songs. As well as Cockney Rejects, other bands that found themselves falling under the banner Oi! in the early days of the genre included The 4-Skins, Angelic Upstarts, The Business, Anti-Establishment, Combat 84, The Blood and Blitz.

The idea behind the Oi! movement was to convey a rough brand of working-class rebellion. Subjects depicted in songs varied from unemployment, workers' rights, oppression by the government, and incessant harassment from the police. Others were less political, with topics including football and street violence, sex and alcohol.

Some fans of Oi! were affiliated with white nationalist organisations such as the National Front and the British Movement, which resulted in some of the media dismissing this subgenre as racist. Yet it must be noted that none of the original Oi! bands such as Angelic Upstarts, The Burial, The Oppressed, and The Business, had not in any way, shape, or form, promoted any form of racism and far-right politics.

However, the white power skinhead movement had steadily developed its own music genre called Rock against Communism (RAC), much of which had similar styles to that of *Oi!*, but was not associated with the Oi! scene. In *Journal of Social History*, author Timothy S. Brown writes:

'"Oi!" played an important symbolic role in the politicization of the skinhead subculture. By providing, for the first time, a musical focus for skinhead identity that was 'white'—that is, that had nothing to do with the West Indian immigrant presence and little obvious connection with black musical roots—Oi! provided a musical focus for new visions of skinhead identity [and] a point of entry for a new brand of right-wing rock music.'

In 1980 when The Cockney Rejects were enjoying chart success with a punk take on the West Ham terrace anthem 'I'm Forever Blowing Bubbles', they played at Birmingham's Cedar Club, a gig which has been described by many as the most violent gig in British history. Jeff Turner, the lead singer of the quartet (then known as "Stinky" Turner) recalled: "I'd seen quite a bit on the terraces or outside football grounds, but this was carnage. There was a lot of people cut and hurt, I got hurt, my brother (Rejects' guitarist Micky Geggus) really got done bad, with an ashtray, the gear was decimated, there was people lying on the floor. Carnage."

The trouble had escalated because of football. Turner: "Most of the punk bands at the time, they had ideals - the Clash, Career Opportunities, political stuff, fair play. When I was a kid, my thought for punk rock was that it could put West Ham on the front pages." Indeed, the group - associated with the club's hooligans in the Inter City Firm - had even appeared on *Top Of the Pops* in West Ham shirts. Turner continued: "After that, everybody wanted to fight us, but you couldn't back down. Once you were defeated, it would have opened the floodgates for everybody...Twenty Cockneys against...well, not all 300 Brummies were trying to attack us, but I'd say we were trying to fight off 50 to 100 people." In the aftermath, Micky Geggus was charged with GBH and affray, thus ending the Cockney Rejects career as a live band. Some months later they attempted to play a gig at Liverpool but it was forced to come to an end after just six songs "because there was 150 Scousers trying to kill us". A later gig at Birmingham was aborted by the police: "At the time, I was gutted, but now, I think 'thank God for that'. Someone could have died."

All of this did little to help the Oi! genre endear itself to the press, and an assessment was once offered by journalist and broadcaster Stuart Maconie: "Punk's stunted idiot half-brother, musically primitive and politically unsavoury, with its close links to far-right groups". On the contrary, Gary Bushell insists that it is "without a doubt, the most misunderstood genre in history."

The main problem really was the fact that Oi! was many of the far-right's soundtrack of choice. Not only did it attract its fair share of football hooligans but also many of the new wave of skinheads - two core groups the NF's direct-action programme targeted for recruitment after they'd lost out at polling stations to Margaret Thatcher. Jeff Turner further remembered: "We played a gig in Camden, we saw these Nazi skinheads beating the shit out of these two punks. They'd managed to wreck Sham 69's career, but us with our following - we weren't going to have it. We just went down and absolutely slaughtered them. We declared to them that if they ever set foot where we were again, we'd decimate them."

Gary Bushell recalled another incident involving the Cockney Rejects: "Neo-nazis confronted the Rejects again at Barking Station. They basically told them 'We're going to come to your gigs, we're going to do this, and we're going to do that.' The Rejects battered them all over the station. They didn't come to the gigs after that." He also pointed out that there was "a Nazi subculture all the way through punk. Malcolm McLaren started it all with the swastikas, which thick people saw and thought, 'Oh, they must be Nazis'" There was an influx of other white power punk bands too, formed by the "Punk Front" division of the National Front. This was really in lieu of real punk bands showing any interest in promoting so-called white supremacy. It was an underhanded trick that the NF were forced to pull again when

Oi! bands rejected any of their invitations - the party had little choice but to recruit a failed punk band from Blackpool called Skrewdriver to become their musical voice of the neo-Nazis movement. Bushell: "It was totally distinct from us. We had no overlap other than a mutual dislike for each other."

When Oi! was at its height, Bushell claims he was a Trotskyist who did his best to infuse the movement with socialist principles. He would organise Oi! conferences and debates which he said was "trying to shape the movement, trying to stop the culture of violence, talking about doing unemployment benefits, working with the Right to Work campaign, prisoners' rights gigs - I thought we could unite punk and social progress...Stinky Turner (Cockney Rejects) was at one debate, and he didn't contribute much, apart from the classic line, 'Oi! is working class, and if you're not working class you'll get a kick in the bollocks.' Perfect! That was what the Rejects were all about." Needless to say, Bushell's latter-day career writing for the likes of the *Sun* and *Daily Star* where he would gleefully provoke the liberal left, did nothing to improve either the public or the media's perceptions regarding Oi!'s political affiliations.

Whether Bushell was a Trotskyist or not, he still managed to fuel further problems, not least by being behind the title of the 1981 compilation *Strength Thru Oi!*. He protested he didn't know, saying "I'd been active in politics for years and had never come across the phrase 'strength through joy' as a Nazi slogan. It was the title of a Skids EP."

Making matters worse, the cover carried a photograph of a skinhead, Nicky Crane, who divided his time between being a neo-Nazi activist and a secret career as a gay porn star! Bushell went on to say on the subject: "I had a Christmas card on the wall, it had that image that was on the cover of *Strength Thru Oi!*, but washed out. I honestly, hand on my heart, thought it was a still from *The Wanderers*. It was only when the album came through for me to approve that I saw his tattoos. Of course, if I hadn't been impatient, I would have said, "right, fucking scrap this, let's shoot something else entirely". Instead, we airbrushed the tattoos out. There were two mistakes there, both mine. Hands up."

There was much worse to follow. In July 1981 an Oi! gig featuring the 4-Skins and the Business in Southall - the scene of a racist murder in 1976 and the race riot that resulted in the death of Blair Peach in 1979 - erupted into sheer violent chaos, with 110 people hospitalised, and the venue, Hambrough Tavern, was petrol bombed. There are a number of conflicting stories regarding this incident, some citing the skinheads as being the cause of the riot after attacking several Asian youths, or Asian youths attacking gig-goers.

According to George Marshall's account in *Spirit of '69: A Skinhead Bible*, the bands had all arrived a couple of hours early in order to do sound checks. The Business were the last to arrive and whose van had come under attack for no apparent reason by a group of Asian youths as it entered the town centre. The driver had ended up having to drive the wrong way down a road to ensure it reached the gig in one piece. By the time of their arrival at the Tavern, there was already a crowd of over 300 Asians on the opposite side of the road, with two dozen policemen keeping an eye on them.

By the time gig-goers arrived at the pub, many recalled having been attacked on their way to the gig, while others had traded verbal abuse. One skinhead recalled that he had been dragged off a bus and brutally assaulted. Others were warned, in no uncertain terms, that they were "going to get it" later on that night.

As the night drew on, the local Asians were expecting - and prepared - for more trouble. With an accumulation of attacks on Asians by skinheads, this had been bubbling for a while. Marshall said the talk on the streets at the time was that if that gig hadn't gone off, then The Meteors' gig booked for the following week would have done. Yet, ironically, The Meteors had neither a skinhead nor a racist following.

According to the press, the arrival of two coaches from the Last Resort didn't do anything to curb the tension. The press claimed that up to six coaches were used, all of which were organised by the National Front. The truth of the matter was that Micky French had booked the coaches, which was simply standard practice when the Last Resort played away and knew its fans would want to travel.

Some of the press even went so far as to say that the coaches all arrived covered in National Front regalia, when in fact the two coaches used by the Last Resort had Union Jack flags in the back window. They speculated that this provoked the locals further.

Marshall goes on to admit that there were some NF and BM supporters at the gig, but so were left wing skinheads, Irish skinheads, and even black skinheads who followed the Last Resort. While the media's propaganda made the public think this was nothing more than a racist gathering, they were, according to Marshall, way off the mark. He goes on to accurately point out that had this been the case then other Oi! bands like The Elite and The Ovaltinies, both of whom pandered to the extreme right, would have been booked as well.

As time went on, the crowd outside the pub grew at an alarming rate - around the two-thousand mark. Even though there was this threat of trouble, a decision was made to allow the gig to go ahead regardless. The opening act was The Business, a group from South London, who had first formed in 1979 and comprised Micky Fitz doing the shouting, Nick Cunningham on drums, Steve Kent on guitar and Martin Smith on bass.

Next up were The Last Resort, already established favourites on the Oi! circuit. They worked their way through a set of crowd-pleasers like 'King of The Jungle' and 'Working Class Kids'. So far, so good; no trouble. Then came the 4-Skins who got the crowd rocking with Oi! classics like 'A.C.A.B' and 'Wonderful World'. However, as the 4-Skins were in the middle of performing 'Chaos', the pub's windows started to smash. Bricks and bottles were raining in on both the police outside and the pub, while the crowd erupted inside, with even the band members and followers grabbing whatever they could to defend themselves.

Soon people were being cut by flying glass before The Tavern was attacked from the rear. Before 11pm that night, the pub doors were unlocked and everybody was evacuated from the building. Many of the skinheads picked up riot shields and stood with the police, in an effort to save the pub and to allow the bands to get all their equipment out. The size of the crowd proved to be too overwhelming and by the time the 4-Skins had just about got everything out, the skinheads and police were forced back beyond the pub. Subsequently a police van was set on fire and then rammed into the pub, seeing it go up in flames.

By this time most of the band's followers were on their way to Hayes & Harlington station. The police sealed off the area, so with the coaches being turned back, the train was the only route home for them. Soon The Special Patrol Group had arrived on the scene, which only hastened to make things worse according to George Marshall: several arrests were made on both sides, the majority being for public order offences. Arthur from the Last Resort was one of them.

The Asians didn't pursue the gig-goers to the station, instead turning their anger at the police and the pub. The Hamborough Tavern was a predominately white pub and this seemed to be the actual target, the Oi! gig seemingly giving them some sort of excuse. The fighting between locals and the police would continue long after the band and their entourage had departed.

One of the members of the 4-Skins recalled his story in the press following the incident. While vehemently denying any association with either the British Movement or National Front movement, he also said how he was forced out by flames and made his way out to the street where he was chased by two "knife wielding" Asian youths. After running a few hundred yards he ran to the nearest house to seek sanctuary. He banged on the door but when it opened the white resident slammed him with a heavy frying pan on his head. Staggering off towards a nearby Black Maria (as at this stage he said he preferred to be arrested than dying), jumped in the back and was welcomed by one of the officers with the words "fascist scum" and a swift boot in the face!

This riot had pretty much drawn Oi's commercial progress to a halt. Turner of the Rejects told *The Guardian* newspaper many years later: "I'd sung a song called 'Oi, Oi, Oi' and all of a sudden there's an Oi! movement and I didn't really want anything to do with it. This awful, awful shit happened in Southall, we were never there, and we got the rug pulled out from under our feet. I went from the TV screen to the labour exchange in 18 months."

After a particularly disparaging article appeared in the *Daily Mail*, Gary Bushell explained: "We never had any problems with Nazi activists at our gigs until after the Mail's piece. Only then did we have people coming back, thinking it was going to be this right-wing thing. When they discovered it wasn't, that's when the trouble started. I was attacked at an Upstarts gig at the 100 Club by about 20 of them. I had a knife pulled on me at Charing Cross station...I had Lars Frederiksen of Rancid come in and sit in the pub round the corner from my house, welling up, telling me if it wasn't for Oi! he might have killed himself as a teenager. I thought, 'Fuck me: it's really had an effect on these people.' I'm not proud of the way Oi! was misunderstood, but I'm proud of the music, proud of what it started, proud of what it gave punk. There were people in 1976 saying punk had to be a Nazi thing because of the swastikas. The difference is, those bands had rock journalists on their side. The Oi! bands only had me. I did me best."

Scooter Skinheads

"People say Lambrettas are unreliable, but they've always been unreliable and that's the fun of having a Lambretta. I mean, these were just a cheap form of transport, but with The Italians the way they style and design everything, it just become an icon...When the northern mod come out, they was sort of a mixture of the mods, the skinheads, everything...and we just loved it....jean jackets, Dr Martens...We were thinking 'Hang on, we can ride scooters and not look like mods'...and that's where the scooter boy thing evolved. For me, it was a way out...When you come from a working class family, just getting away from ya mom and dad constantly arguing...EVERY rally was like a party."
--Mick Gauntlett - Surrey Scooter Services

By the mid-1980s, all was quiet was on the skinhead front. 2 Tone was a fading memory and Oi! had just about gone. Had it not been for the scooter rallies, the skinhead scene would have become virtually extinct.

The mod culture had never completely disappeared and its spirit was alive and kicking in the North of England, due to many soul all-nighters and scooter clubs. Wigan Casino had kept its doors open for northern soul lovers up until 1981, and by the end could still boast having 80,000 members. Now, many will say was that the Casino was far from glamorous. The peeling paint and toilets that were ankle deep in piss was all brushed aside; the main thing was to hit the dancefloor and put your feet where your soul was. It's actually been noted that in the States you couldn't give away soul records and they were often then shipped to Britain to sell for next to nothing. Yet this didn't stop the rarest of collectable vinyl selling up to a thousand pounds apiece.

Central to the northern soul scene were the array of scooter clubs. Nearly every town in Lancashire and Yorkshire had its own scooter club, some having up to 200 devoted members. In the 1970s, clubs would often go on weekend rallies to the coast, and by the end of the decade they had transformed into massive rallies, all courtesy of the mod revival.

These numbers dropped significantly when plastic mods had dis-covered a new craze to follow, yet the scooter fraternity was, in a way, stronger than it had been in years. Many scooter-ists abandoned the mod look and the runs became more of a gathering of general enthuse-iasts rather any than being more concerned with a particular fashion.

By the 1980s numbers were on the increase again, with new clubs opening all over Britain. The rallies rapidly became more of an alliance of youth cults rather than a mod preserve, and campsites became the temporary home for several skinheads, mods, psychobillies, and scooterists.

The scooter skins had been part of the northern scene since the dawn of the seventies, although these were only in fairly small numbers. However, by 1984 all of the major clubs such as the Mansfield Monsters, The Soldiers of Fortune, The Mercenaries and the Stafford Boro Upsetters all could claim to having large numbers of skinheads. There were even skinhead only clubs with names such as the Cardiff Cougars, the Birmingham Bulldogs and the Union Jack Club from Cumbria.

The scooter scene was completely ignored by the mainstream media, but soon became the focus of all things street. Bank Holiday rallies could attract anything up to 15,000 people. For the bigger rallies, entertainment would be laid on in the form of dances and live bands. Such events would attract even greater numbers, although some of those in attendance would be no more than hangers-on and having no genuine interest in scooters other than cadging a lift on the back of mates to and from the rally. Some didn't even bother to turn up to rallies by scooter, instead travelling by car, van or train.

Inevitably, trouble was never far away and by 1985 thieving had become a serious concern. Customised and chromed parts were being stolen away regularly, as well as costly exhausts, side panels, and spare wheels; basically anything the thief could lay their hands on. If anything could be loosed by a spanner or screwdriver, you could guarantee someone would steal it, and failing that, the whole scooter itself would be stolen.

Where there was aggro you could safely say the skinheads were never far away. In 1984 at Kewick, trouble had ensued when somebody threw a few petrol bombs in the direction of police in attendance. This, however, was nothing compared to another event.

It was in 1986 and the first rally of the year was during Easter weekend at Great Yarmouth. For the 6,500 scooterists, everything had gone well until the Sunday night. Ska legend Desmond Dekker was performing at a local nightclub called Tiffany's. Everyone was having a ball and the place was packed to the rafters. Until Dekker started performing his #1 hit classic 'Israelites' and disaster struck. Over 30 National Front skinheads stormed the stage, in what was obviously a planned attack that security had not anticipated. The whole pack gave Dekker a beating, lashed out at other scooterists before running out the club altogether. However, it transpired that some members of the security team were actually National Front supporters themselves, and to those present it looked certain that that they had been a part of this planned attack, although other security officers did their best to maintain order during this unexpected stage invasion.

Even worse was to come, though, during the August bank holiday weekend on the Isle of Wight. This has always been one of the most popular and well attended rallies and 1986 was to prove no exception. On the Saturday night all was well, with Motown legend Edwin Starr providing the entertainment. On the Sunday night, the entertainment bill included The Business, Condemned 84 and Vicious Rumours. These were all renowned acts on the Oi! Scene, but weren't particular favourites of some scooterists. However, everything went off without a hitch and no trouble came.

By the early hours of the Monday morning trouble began when a few people decided to turn over the beer tent. The owner had already ripped off all those in attendance, and before long many other scooterists joined in the overturning of the beer tent, helping themselves to all his stock. Nobody was too concerned about this until someone decided to burn down the tent. Before anyone knew it, the whole tent had gone up in flames and gas cylinders had exploded.

If that wasn't bad enough, some of the scooterists turned their attention to the food stalls and the other traders' stalls, even though many of them were actually run by fellow scooterists. Anyone who dared try and protect their stock were attacked, and even the fire brigade had missiles thrown at them. Then certain groups of scooterists went around punching anyone they didn't like the look of, or who looked shifty.

Tabloid tales of "mods versus Hell's Angels battles" circulated the next day, though none of it had really affected the general public, with all trouble being confined to the campsite. This was the reason why scooter rallies were able to continue.

In 1987 it was decided to make the campsites open to National Run Committee members only and to ban any live bands, all in an effort to get back to the days of scooter riders-only rallies. Many traditional skinheads, who wanted to distance themselves from the boneheads that had given the scene such a bad name, even started going to mod rallies.

Today, much of the violence and the thieving has been stamped out, with rallies continuing to enthral many. And it looks set to continue for many more years to come. The unprovoked attack on a legend like Desmond Dekker highlighted how some sections of the skinhead subculture had drifted from its roots. Many traditional skinheads do their upmost to preserve their culture and fly the traditional skinhead flag.

Skinhead Films

At the height of the original skinhead subculture, a series of novels were written by Richard Allen (his real name was James Moffatt), depicting the fictitious adventures of Joe Hawkins and his friends. While causing an uproar with the media, his first book *Skinhead* sold over a million copies. The controversy surrounding these books only seemed to fuel sales, and his follow-up, *Suedehead*, first published in 1971 and finding Joe Hawkins released from prison and his discovery that the cult had moved on, also would sell over a million copies.

The central character, Joe, was violent, racist, and sexist, and when he wasn't "having it off" with some bird, was beating the crap out of someone, or planning some sort of robbery. While these novels were very popular in their time, Allen widely regarded as the king of pulp fiction, these books did little to improve the already-bad reputation the skinhead scene had.

In 1971, Stanley Kubrick's *A Clockwork Orange* really struck a chord with skinheads, and sparked controversy elsewhere. Based on Anthony Burgess' book of the same name, it was a story of extreme violence and the freedom of choice. Coming hot on the heels of another controversial film, *Straw Dogs*, the film was forced to be edited by censors, while some local councils went as far as banning it altogether. Kubrick eventually withdrew the film with rumours circulating that he had received numerous death threats, but it was actually because he refused to make further edits to it.

Skinheads were instantly drawn to this tale, while on the other hand the media made claims that *A Clockwork Orange* was inciting trouble and every act of violence was labelled a "clockwork crime". The main character is Alex Delarge (Malcolm McDowell), who leads a gang of thugs who go on

115

a horrific crime spree. Alex winds up incarcerated and is set free on the condition that he undergoes a new cure for criminals. This involves him having to take brainwashing drugs which makes him instantly sick if he even thinks of violence and sex. While his behaviour drastically improves, many liberals believe Alex is being denied the freedom of choice, and the story continues with Alex being used as a political guinea pig.

Alex and his group of thugs were dressed in a mixture of city gentleman smartness and the bootboy gear of the day. The film influenced many that had been involved in the skinhead subculture to attend football matches dressed in white boiler suits, black boots and bowler hats, and then following the game fight with their opponents.

A Clockwork Orange remains one of the most popular underground films of all time and its influence among many skinhead bands is evident, including with the likes of Blitz, The Violators, and The Clockwork Soldiers. The cover sleeve to The Upstart's 'Teenage Warning' featured an orange on it with a key through it and The Last Resort recorded 'Horrorshow' as The Warriors. The band who really acknowledged the film more than any other was undoubtedly The Addicts. They dressed the part, including singer Monkey's painted face, played punk versions of the classical music that Alex loves, and even went so far as to call one of their albums *Smart Alex.*

Over the years, there have been a number of British films made revolving around skinhead culture. Obviously like anything, some of the films are better than others. In April 1982, *Oi! For England* was screened by ITV, a made-for-TV film written in response to the riots of the early 1980s, and not to mention the alarming rise in neo-Nazism in the same period. With a screenplay by Trevor Griffiths', many could argue this film is just as relevant today as it was back in 1982.

Riots in Bristol, Liverpool, Brixton, and elsewhere, all had disparate triggers, but were mainly fuelled by the anger at the mass youth unemployment, hopelessness, poverty, oppressive policing and racism, all of which were blamed on Margaret Thatcher's economics. The film is set in Moss Side, Manchester - which had been the scene of its own riots in the summer of 1981 - Griffiths' play is centred on four skinheads, all of whom have aspirations to become musicians. The four gather in a dusty basement to release their frustrations by way of violent, angry songs played on ripped-off instruments. There's the hot-headed Napper (Neil Pearson), dopey Swells (Ian Mercer), Landry (Richard Platt), and the eldest and most sensitive, Finn (Adam Kotz), the group's songwriter. They call themselves Ammunition and the band play raucous Oi! music. A race riot occurs outside and the band is offered a chance to perform at a 'skinfest', a front for a fascist rally. The four ambitious lads find their loyalties tested.

This compelling play proved so popular that it transferred to the stage, touring youth clubs and community theatres in an attempt to unite working-class audiences against fascism. While the film is relatively obscure these days, it's worth seeking out online, and audiences that saw this film upon its original transmission will no doubt remember this with great affection. Here, the portrayal of characters were real, honest and the writing well-structured, not simply just portraying skinheads as one-dimensional racist thugs, which, unfortunately, much of the media had painted them to be. It was refreshing to see real skinheads being separated from the bonehead Nazis.

The following year in 1983, another excellent British television play was screened by ITV, *Made in Britain*. Written by David Leyland and directed by Alan Clarke, the film centres on a 16-year-old racist skinhead named Trevor, played by a young Tim Roth, who turns in a powerful, nuanced performance. Contrary to being a racist, Trevor is bright and articulate, though he is a habitual offender, constantly being sent to institutions, and following his latest arrest, the authorities struggle to deal with him, all of which delights him. He believes he can beat the system by belligerence and defiance and sees himself as the victim of authoritarianism.

In preparation for his role, Tim Roth would attend many National Front meetings in order to make his performance as authentic as possible. Following its original screening, it caused a wave of controversy, even from tabloids like the *Sun*. Tim Roth said in an interview years later about such disparaging reviews by the media: "I mean, you know... "How dare you make a film about a racist?" Well, if we don't make any films about these people does that mean it doesn't exist? We can all go and hide? What are you supposed to do, make picture postcard films? I don't understand that mentality. I suppose it was Thatcher's mentality in a way. Crush the critic."

That same year, Tim Roth also starred alongside Phil Daniels and Gary Oldman in the acclaimed Channel 4 film, *Meantime*. Directed by Mike Leigh, it was first shown at the London Film Festival in 1983 before being aired by Channel 4 a few weeks later. One of the critics at the Festival, Michael Coveney, said, 'The sapping, debilitating and demeaning state of unemployment, the futile sense of waste, has not been more poignantly or poetically expressed in any other film of the period.'

Meantime is another gritty, realistic look at Thatcher's Britain in the 1980s. The film is centred on a working-class family in London's East End who are struggling to survive during the recession and have all but given up on life in general. Tim Roth plays the timid Colin, who looks up to racist skinhead Coxy, played by Gary Oldman. Eventually Colin shaves his head in order to become a skinhead like his friend.

There were a number of international skinhead films through the 1980s and 90s, one of them notably being *Romper Stomper*, an Australian drama starring Russell Crowe, and directed by Geoffrey Wright, which depicts a dark tale of the exploits and downfalls of a neo-Nazis group in blue collar suburban Melbourne. Another skinhead film of note was the American crime-drama *American History X*, a film written by David McKenna, and boasting a stellar cast with Edward Norton and Edward Furlong in the leading roles. The film depicts two brothers who become involved in the neo-Nazi movement. Following the older brother serving three years in prison for voluntary manslaughter, he comes out completely reformed, and tries in vain to guide his younger brother away from the neo-Nazi movement.

One of the most acclaimed skinheads films of all time came in 2006, *This Is England*, written and directed by Shane Meadows. Meadows based the film on his own real-life experiences as a young skinhead in the early 1980s. The film shrewdly illustrates how the skinhead subculture was hijacked by white nationalists, leading to a divide of the whole skinhead scene. The film's title is a reference to a line Combo (Stephen Graham) uses during one of his speeches when explaining his nationalist views.

The film explores how 12-year-old Shaun (Thomas Turgoose) joins a gang of friendly, multi-cultural skinheads led by Woody (Joseph Gilgunn). They become like a surrogate family for the young boy who is still grieving the loss of his father who had died in the Falklands War. After a prison sentence, Combo returns to the group. He expresses English nationalist and racist views and attempts to enforce leadership over the other skinheads. Woody and his gang are having none of it, none of whom share his racist views, leading to the gang splitting up. The young, naive Shaun ends up going off with Combo and his friends and before long he's off to white nationalist meetings with him. After Shaun's friend, Milky (Andrew Shim), the only black skinhead of the group, is badly beaten up by Combo, he realises he is not really racist and should never have left Woody and the gang.

Adding to the winning ingredients of this film is the sizzling ska and reggae soundtrack that accompanies some of the scenes, which includes '54-46 Was My Number' by Toots & The Maytals (now a heralded skinhead anthem), 'Louie Louie', also by the Maytals and 'Return of Django' by Lee "Scratch" Perry & The Upsetters.

This coming-of-age story set in 1983 mirrors Shane Meadows' own experiences as a 12-year-old, where he had briefly fell in with a racist crowd. Meadows recalled his story for an article in *The Guardian*:

"It's easy to laugh at the 1980s. Many people base their memories on the stuff they see in those I Love the 80s TV shows: massive VHS recorders, Atari consoles and rubbish digital watches, all shown against a backing of Now That's What I Call Music Vol 2. Then there was the way that people dressed: your mum with a deranged perm, your dad in a pair of grey leather slip-ons and your sister with a "Frankie Says Relax" T-shirt and a stack of love bites round her neck.

"But my memories have more meaning than that. As a kid growing up in Uttoxeter, Staffs, it was a time of great music, brilliant fashion and a vibrant youth culture that makes today's kids look dull and unimaginative by comparison. It was also a time of massive unrest when British people were still prepared to fight for the stuff they believed in. My new film, *This Is England*, is about all of these things.

"Set in 1983, this is the first period film I have made. A great deal of it is based on my own childhood and I tried to recreate my memoirs of being an 11-year-old kid trying to fit in. It was a time when Uttoxeter, like the rest of the country, was awash with endless different youth tribes.

There were new romantics, heavy rockers, smoothies, punks, goths, skins and mod revivalists who were into the Specials and 2 Tone. Then there were those pop culture kids who came into school wearing one green sock, one pink sock and some deely boppers on their head. People often looked daft, but were genuinely committed to their chosen denomination and would wear their identities on their sleeves with immense pride. In a town as small as Uttoxeter, though, there weren't enough people for each sub culture to fill their own parties or clubs, so most weekends everyone would turn up at the same village hall disco and end up fighting.

"Like most 11-year-old kids who wore jumpers with animals on, I got bullied by the older kids at school. So I looked for my own tribe to join. It was the skinhead movement that enamoured me the most. I remember seeing 10 or 15 of them at the bus shelter on my way home from school one summer night and thinking they were the most fearsome thing I had ever seen. Even though I was terrified of them, I was instantly attracted to them. To be a part of most of the other factions you had to be a little rich kid. But to be a skinhead, all you needed was a pair of jeans, some work boots, a white shirt and a shaved head. You could be transformed from a twerp into a fearsome warrior in 15 minutes. Skins appealed to me because they were like soldiers: they wore their outfits like suits of armour and demanded respect. There were playground myths that surrounded them and especially their Dr Martens boots. It was feared that a single kick from a DM boot would kill you or at the very least give you brain damage. I can remember kids refusing to fight unless the skinhead agreed to remove his fearsome boots first.

"My older sister was going out with a skinhead who took me under his wing and taught me about the roots of the whole culture. He was a nice bloke who bore no relation to the stereotypical racist yob that people now associate with that time. It was him that I based the character of Woody on in the film. I learned from him that skinheads had grown out of working class English lads working side by side with West Indians in factories and shipyards in the late-60s. The black lads would take the whites to blues parties where they were exposed to ska music for the first time. Soon Jamaican artists like Desmond Dekker, the Upsetters, and Toots and the Maytals were making a living out of songs aimed directly at English white kids. This was where the whole skinhead thing came from - it was inherently multicultural. But nowadays when I tell people that I used to be a skinhead, they think I'm saying I used to be racist. My film shows how right-wing politics started to creep into skinhead culture in the 1980s and change people's perception of it. This was a time when there were three and a half million people unemployed and we were involved in a pointless war in the Falklands. When people are frustrated and disillusioned that's when you get extremist groups moving in and trying to exploit the situation. That's what the National Front did in the early-80s.

"Skinheads had always taken pride in being working class and English, so they were easy targets for the NF who said that their identities were under threat. They cultivated a real hatred of the Asian community. In the film, Combo represents the sort of charismatic leader the NF used to turn skinheads into violent street enforcers. Suddenly, all skinheads were branded the same way. But most of the real old skins who were into the music and the clothes went on to be scooter boys to separate themselves from the racism. I always wanted *This Is England* to tell the truth about skinheads.

"As I started to make the film, other themes started to interest me. We had a relatively small budget so we couldn't afford to recreate every last detail of the Uttoxeter of 1983. Instead, I set the scene by using archive news footage at the start and end of the film. Going through footage of the Falklands War really made me think again about the whole thing. As kids, we thought it was like going into a World Cup campaign. It was exciting and we were cheering on our lads to go and do the Argies. But the scenes of soldiers' coffins shocked and appalled me.

"In many ways the country was a mess. The miners' strike was massive - they were killing scabs by throwing paving slabs from bridges onto cars. You had all the protesters and unrest at Greenham Common. But remembering all of these things made me nostalgic for a time when people were ready to stand up and say something. People cared about where the country was going. As the 1980s ended we had the poll tax riots which turned out to be the end of an era. Afterwards, it was like the nation lost its backbone. People were bought off. They were given a little bit of land, the right to buy their council house and put a little satellite dish on the front of it. They became content and lost their will to rock the boat.

"The big difference between now and the period in which my film is set is our level of isolation. In 1983 people still cared about society as a whole but now they'll keep their mouth shut as long as they've got the house, the job and the car they want. If you were a kid in 1983, you wouldn't have a PlayStation to sit indoors alone with. You got your entertainment from mixing with a variety of different people.

While making the film I realised that all of my fondest childhood memories surrounded human contact: mucking about with mates or going camping. In 2007, people put less emphasis on that sort of thing and more on planning their careers and their TV viewing. As far as I'm concerned, if you're working from nine to five then coming home to watch shows that your Sky box has recorded for you while you were out, you might as well be on a fucking drip.

"This Is England is a snapshot of an era and a life that seems very dated now. It's about sticking up for mates and beliefs."

It was refreshing for a skinhead film to show the different types of skinheads. The first gang of skinheads the young Shaun finds himself part of are friendly, warm, compassionate and very much like a family, mirroring real skinhead culture. It then makes way for the darker side when Combo and his gang arrive, accurately conveying how there had become a big divide between real skinheads and the invasion of Nazi boneheads who invaded the scene, and, in turn, blackened the whole culture in the media and general public even more than it already was.

The film was a resounding success, winning the Alexander Korda Award for Best British Film at the 2007 British Academy Film Awards, Best Film at the 2006 British Independent Film Awards and the immensely talented Thomas Turgoose deservedly winning the Most Promising Newcomer Award.

Skinheads Groups

There were many skinhead-related subcultures. In the early 1980s the casuals was born, a subsection of association football that is essentially typified by football hooliganism. The dress code was all expensive designer clothing (referred to as "clobber") such as Stone Island, CP Company and Lacoste, all in an effort to avoid the attention of police and to intimidate their rivals. Some casuals would actually wear clothes that are vastly similar to those worn by the mods. Casuals were depicted in films such as *The Football Factory, ID* and *The Firm.*

The designer clothing and fashion aspect of casuals had begun in 1977-78. According to Nicky Allt, a well-documented precursor was the trend to Liverpool youths starting to wear different clothing to other football fans, such as Peter Storm jackets, straight-leg jeans and Adidas trainers. The first British football fans to wear continental Europe fashions were Liverpool F.C fans. These were usually bought while they'd be following their teams at matches in Europe.

A precursor to casuals were known as the Perry Boys, originating in the mid-1970s. This subculture had consisted of Manchester football hooligans styling their hair into a flick and their dress code being sportswear, like Fred Perry shirts and Dunlop Green Flash trainers.

The casual style and subculture initially had no name, widely considered as a *smart* look. It evolved in the early 80s, becoming a huge subculture, and characterised by expensive sportswear brands such as Fila, Tacchini and Diadora.

Several years later a group called Casuals United, also referred to as UK Casuals United, was formed in 2009. This is a British anti-Islamic protest group and is closely affiliated with the English Defence League, a far-right street protest movement which opposes what they perceive as the spreading of Islamism, Sharia law and Islamic extremism in England.

Proving that not all skinheads are racist thugs, an anti-racist and anti-fascist group called SHARP (Skinheads against Racial Prejudice) had been formed in the UK in the late 1960s. SHARPS deeply resent the racial hijacking of the skinhead name by white power skinheads - who are usually referred to as "boneheads". The SHARP logo is based on the famous Trojan Records' logo, a label that released mainly black Jamaican ska, rocksteady and reggae recordings. Other than the issue of anti-racism, there is actually no other official political ideology of SHARP.

Soulboys was another UK subculture, largely associated with the skinheads. This was at its most prominent in the late 1970s and early 1980s, and comprised of ardent lovers of American soul and funk music. It emerged in North-West England as northern soul attendees had begun to take more interest in the modern funk and jazz sounds of artists like Roy Ayers and Lonnie Liston Smith, instead of the obscure 1960s soul records that had largely characterised the northern soul scene.

There was a significant development of the subculture at nightclubs such as The Goldmine in Canvey Island and The Royalty in Southgate. A number of DJs were prominently associated with the Soulboy scene, including Robbie Vincent, Greg Edwards, Chris Hill, Pete Tong and Chris Bangs. Caister Soul Weekenders became highly popular and one of the main features of the subculture, and still exists to this day. Heavily influenced by the soulboys were the casual subculture that had emerged in the 1980s, which included the sideways fringed wedge hairstyle. As the soulboy scene was largely working-class and revolved around their love of American funk and soul acts, they received far less media coverage than some of the more middle-class youth cultures of the day, most notably included the new romantics.

A redskin, in context of the skinhead subculture, is a socialist, communist, or anarchist skinhead. The redskins take a militant anti-fascist and pro-working class stance. Red and Anarchist Skinheads, known as RASH, the SHARPs, Anti -Fascist Action and Red Action are all the most well-known organisations associated with redskins.

Trojan Skinheads, also known as traditional skinheads or trads, is made up of individuals who identify with the original British skinhead subculture of the late 1960s. They are named after the famous record label Trojan, and identify with the British working class mod roots and the music of the original skinhead like ska, reggae, rocksteady and soul.

In their appreciation of black music, they are totally the opposite of white power skinheads, and, therefore, are totally against such racism as depicted by this group. Trojans wear the traditional skinhead clothes such as button-down Ben Sherman shirts, Fred Perry polo shirts, braces, fitted suits, Harrington jackets (this style of jacket earned the nickname Harrington as it was worn by Ryan O'Neal's character, Harrington, in the 1960s American soap opera Peyton Place), cardigans, tank tops, and Crombie-style overcoats. In contrast to the shorter-hair, punk-influenced Oi! skins of the 1980s, hair is generally between a 2 and 4 grade clip guard.

Spirit of '69 is a phrase used by traditional skinheads as a nod to the original subculture's movement. The phrase was originally popularised by the Glasgow Spy Kids, a group of Scottish skinheads and two of the Spy Kids appear on the cover of *Spirit of '69: A Skinhead Bible'* by author George Marshall (he, too, was a skinhead from Glasgow).

Skinhead Stories

The following are accounts from various skinheads from different eras. Some are fairly straight-forward and adhere to what being a skinhead is all about. Others may shock. In no way is this any glorification of violence, it is just skinheads telling it how it was, in their own words, and each paint a vivid picture of what it was like being a skinhead. There are one or two stories that completely contradict themselves, but then, as I mentioned earlier, EVERY subculture is a mass of contradictions.

DAVE EALAND

Photo © Dave Ealand

My initial introduction to the skinhead world was on one Thursday evening in July 1979 whilst watching *Top of the Pops* (something I did religiously). It was when watching this particular edition that a new band was introduced, The Specials, who were performing their current single 'Gangsters'. I remember being completely enthralled by the group, just loving this new sound I was hearing. The following day at school this great new band and sound was the talk of the playground, especially among my mates and I. This sparked off a trend amongst us; within just a few weeks we all had our Harringtons, Doc Martens and braces, blatantly trying to imitate what we had seen on TV.

132

It was around the same time when there came a whole new wave of fantastic two tone groups, and by Christmas 1979 I was well on my way with several purchases from my local record shop; Desmond Dekker, Dave & Ansell Collins and so many others boomed from my new stereo. There it all began. Even now I love to collect 2 Tone, ska and reggae music, mainly on vinyl.

Photo © Dave Ealand

I have been DJ'ing at ska & reggae events for many years now from my growing vinyl collection which also contains many Soul/Northern Soul and Motown records. An annual skinhead event is held in Margate (known as Skagate) during the summer, in which I DJ and I have so many great, great memories and have made a lot of close mates over the years. That's what being a skinhead is for me; it's all about looking smart, having good skin-mates, good music, good beer and bloody good times! It saddens me that some have this misconception that if you're a skinhead, you automatically must be a thug and a racist. It's so not true. I think a lot of this stems from the propaganda in the media, where they often sensationalise a story to make it better reading. Shame they had to label us all as one, as that isn't the case. Far from it. For the traditional skinhead, the scene is about the music and looking smart.

Unfortunately, there were other groups of skinheads that emerged over the years that took it out of context and saw being a skinhead as a way to scare and intimidate people and to enforce their racist and political views upon the world, particularly those associated with the National Front and the BNP. Us real skinheads refer to them as "boneheads" and SCUM! So, as I said, at the heart of the skinhead culture, which is a multi-cultural scene, is the mutual love of the music that helped shape the whole scene, the fashion, and unity. Yes, I do get annoyed when I've been accused of being a racist just because of the way I look, but if I think they are worth educating then I will take the time to explain to them the very big difference.

KIM KEANIE

I'm now in my 50s and I'm still a proud Skinhead girl. As a child I was brought up in care. I was 14 when I first became a skinhead girl. To me, those on the scene were my real family and I no longer felt alone. I eventually ran away from care and went to live in Brighton with my skinhead family. To me being a skinhead is about belonging to a universal family, taking pride in being a skinhead and respect for others. Also, in 2017 I shall be getting married in skinhead style!

HARRY BRASS

I was once asked what makes a "Skinhead". Is it cropped hair? Is it Dr Marten Boots? Is it Ben Sherman shirts and 501's? While they are all a part of it, there is so much more. The music is a huge part for me. The music really speaks to my soul. Original Ska, Skinhead Reggae, Rocksteady, Lovers Rock and 2 Tone (which I collect on vinyl) really push my buttons.

All of these things and even more go into being a skinhead. It's an attitude (not necessarily "being hard", though I can take a smack up the chops just as well as I can dish them out!); It's the pride in being well turned-out with my Docs polished, jeans turned up (to show off the boots), 3 finger collar on my shirt and Fred Perry jumper on my back, topped off with a Harrington/Crombie and Porkpie or Trilby on my "napper" (head).

It's the pride I feel when original skins/hard mods (from back in the day) come up to me to tell me my look is "TIGHT". It's passing another Skin and knowing that their look is as sharp (as in dressed) as mine. Real Skinheads the world over know what it is to be a Skin: You certainly don't need loads of money; you just need the spark in your heart and a clean look (whether your jeans cost £10 or 100). Keep the Faith and be the best Skin you can be, because every time you're out you're not just representing yourself but representing the scene, including those who have gone before.

Hold your head up high, be proud and carry the 40 plus years of culture with you!

BERNARD NUGENT

 I'm 43 years old and have been a skinhead for over 20 yrs. It was the Specials 7" single 'The Skeleton at The Keyboard' that initially sparked my interest. I used to sneak into my big brother's room and play this single on his record player.

Gerry, my big brother, was a mod and was 7 years older than me. He'd seen that I'd taken a keen interest in the Specials and he would talk to me about the music; that's how I found 2 TONE. When realising they were doing certain cover version of songs, I decided to check out the Trojan records originals, all of which totally blew me away!!!! Also I have to say that I love the look of skinhead girls.

I can remember once being stopped by two young lads in a pub: One was a black deaf lad and his white mate would translate for him. He asked "You're a SKINHEAD, right?" I answered "Yes mate, that's right!" I couldn't believe it when his response was "You must hate black people right?" My immediate reply was, "No! Half of my culture is Jamaican!" They both just looked bemused. I then showed them my tattoo that explains the origins of SKINHEAD culture.... They then both apologised and each bought me a beer each and referred to me as "BROTHER ".

BOB WELLER

I suppose at first the reason I became a skinhead was because it was a way to rebel against the system; a system that was just not working for the working class. We were all trying to find our identity and I know that I wanted to discover who I really was. I knew I was no punk and even though I liked some of the music, the punk scene was too scruffy for me. Us skinheads loved ska music. Christmases and birthdays were the chances to get some decent clobber. To be honest, I stole the first Harrington I ever had from the coat rack at school. Not something I'm proud of. I was just a young kid trying to grow up in the Thatcher years, living on a run-down council estate in Telford, Shropshire. It was bleak. There wasn't much in the way of hope or encouragement. Both parents were on the dole and as my dad would often say, we didn't have "2 brass tacks". Believe me, we really didn't! It was a terrible time for all of us growing up on that estate. We used to spend a lot of our spare time glue-sniffing or gas-sniffing down the subway or in the woods. It was just a cheap and easy way of getting high.

Certainly the pack I knocked about with were not racist. We had our mate, Ian, who was like our Rude Boy and he was the one who always managed to get a Crombie or a Harrington first. We would always look out for Ian, as because he was black he used to often get called names, especially by the older lot. And I mean parents and elders who should have known better! I even got a few slaps off my dad once for bringing him round my house! Yep even my old man never liked "darkies", as he called them, and it caused a bit of a rift between Dad and I. He was ex-forces and had served all over the world, yet he would only really trust someone if they were white and English. If anyone would shout racist abuse at our mate Ian – which was frequent - we would give these people loads of grief back. Often they'd be bigger than us and there could be as many as a dozen of them.

We generally felt unwanted; we were like the jilted generation. The only way we got something back then was if we stole it. We used to go and steal from shops and sometimes we had it down to an art form. That was the way it was; we certainly couldn't afford scooters and the majority of time the bus was out as well so it was shanks' pony (walking everywhere) for us. The first Vespa I ever rode I had stolen. I know I'm not proud of the fact now but hey, we had fuck all at the time and nobody gave a toss about us so it was a type of "fuck you" attitude to the world (and I figure I have had enough bad karma to even things out a bit).

It was around the time of the People's March for Jobs in the early 1980s that we got into football. We would go and watch Birmingham City whose crew became the Zulu's. It was then that we started to channel our anger and hatred into violence. I mean, we had seen the miners' strike on TV so we thought it was all OK, really. We never give it to anyone who wasn't up for it themselves. One time when Birmingham

City was playing against Notts Forrest, we all had a bit of a scrap outside the ground and then got split up from the mob. Later that day, as Ian and I were making our way to our guys' meeting place, all of a sudden some Forest fans pulled up in a car and there was four of them. They started giving Ian loads of racial abuse so I started to mouth back at them. Up until that point in my life I had never seen anyone pull a knife, but all these guys had blades on them. We stood, frozen for a bit, shocked more than anything, but eventually took to our heels and ran for our lives. Of course they pursued us but we managed to get to the meet up place where our lads were waiting for us and thankfully that was just down the road. We finally caught up with the rest of the crew just as the Ford Capri with the four Forest fans arrived, windows shut and all quiet. I can only figure they saw all us together and thought better of it. Ian then shouted, "There's the cunts that tried to stab us!" From there it all escalated. For trying to stab me and Ian, the crew decided the best way to teach them a lesson they'd never forget was to break all of their fingers, and that's exactly what we did! After this massive fight we then burned their car! They never bothered us again, I can tell you that much!

There were many good times being a skinhead. There was togetherness. It was a massive part of my life. I do have to live with the guilt of some of the things we did back then but I think I've had my karma back now. Today I live a totally different lifestyle, one that's far more reserved now I'm a family man, but seriously I wouldn't change much even if I could. I maybe wouldn't have stolen that guy's scooter and drove it into the lake, even though I never got caught for that... But mainly those were good times, it was fun and a way of feeling that we were standing up and being counted against all the odds.

STEVE BAWDEN

 At the tender age of 14 my best friend Steve and I were both trying to decide which road to travel down. Should we be Mods? Rockers? Hippies/Wallys? Or Skinheads? Hippies/Wallys was crossed off the list with ease so we continued to review the remaining three.

It was during one Saturday that we both decided to set off on an adventure. Both being keen Chelsea fans we thought "Right, let's get up to Stamford Bridge!" We had very limited money so we purchased a platform ticket at Chatham station, went onto the London bound side and jumped on a train. Once there, we managed to dodge our way to the ground and, with the help of a group of chaps, we slid under the turnstiles and onto the terraces all for a couple of pennies. The sight we saw left us both dumbstruck; an army of Skinheads. That day sealed our fate; we were two future Skinheads in the making.

We both went on money-making missions, many of them being slightly beyond the law but nothing was going to stop us as far as we were concerned. First off came our hair. That proved to be a bit of a shock, for not only us two but most of the people around us. The clothing was always going to be hard to come by so I did two paper rounds a day, plus I helped a family friend on his bakers round for cash and I did fruit picking through the summer holidays. I got my Doc Martens for going out and about in and a pair of Squires royal brogues for school. There was no turning back from that point. The trend seemed to be picking up at an alarming rate, which was pretty damn cool.

I stayed on at school for the 5th year (which wasn't compulsory then). We were allowed to design our own uniform, as by then we pretty much ran the school as semi pro-bullies. We decided what the uniform would be: A Black blazer with chrome buttons, bottle -green Levi Sta-Prest, white button-down shirt and a slim black tie with a small white Invicta horse on it. Yes it was probably the best school uniform in the country!

We would often visit a record shop called Disco Two, plus another two record stores in Chatham High Street. The chap who ran the store would have a delivery of Jamaican imports once a week. We would both stand in the record booth and make our selections. These records would be going to the school disco. Leading up to school disco night about 8 of us would go to Steve's house (he had a massive bedroom), play our favourite tunes and practice our Skinhead Reggae dancing so that on the night we would all be dancing in perfect step with each other. We thought we were the dog's dangly bits!

During the last term of our 5th year we were all flat out taking apprenticeship entry exams to secure our futures, along with, of course, GCSE exams. I ended up passing every entry exam I had taken which gave me the welcome choice of five different apprenticeships. My choice was H M Naval base Chatham. My main reason for this choice was so I could get my hands (or should I say feet) on a pair of Dockers safety shoes. These wonderful shoes were made by Dr Marten, commissioned by the M O D to make them and were only available from the Navy bases around the country. They were 6602's at the safety clothing store; I've never forgotten that number as I was doing a roaring trade selling them.

For a short spell a group of us wore white combat trousers, which we managed to fiddle from the bakers in Strood by way of the chap that I'd helped out on his bakers round. They looked rather nice with oxblood boots, slightly encouraged by the film *A Clockwork Orange* (though we left the eye make-up and bowler hats out of it!).

I managed to purchase myself a Mohair & Trevira tonic suit from Rochester Market. The chap had hundreds of them in all available colours and he sold on a pick and mix basis. My choice was turquoise blue and gold and the colour change was unbelievable. I got myself my first checked shirt to compliment it (most shirts were candy striped prior to that) in a pale blue and brown large gingham check and that was the only shirt I've ever managed to actually wear right out. It was see-through eventually and at that point my mum refused to wash it anymore, bless it.

Our local watering hole was The George in Rochester High St. I'd been drinking there from the age of 15 (naughty boy). I would describe it as a scooter skins venue with loads of scooters and loads of skinheads. On the other side of Rochester Bridge in Strood was The Prince of Wales pub just about 700 yards away. This was the basecamp for a gang of what we called Greebo's (rockers or Greasers). We had on-going aggravation with them. They could always hear us coming like a swarm of bees and we would always oblige them with an R A F style fly past. They would try to kick our panels in, so in return we would shower them with missiles. It was semi-friendly fire as we never actually came to blows with them. We did, however, set up one fight: we had a chap called Kipper and the Greebo's had a chap called Malcolm, both of whom were polio sufferers and both had leg callipers. They had upper body strength second to none! This was an epic battle/slogging match as neither man would give up and we all would have a beer together after the fight.

The Medway towns where I was born (and still reside) had the highest violent crime rate in the country for many years, beginning in the early 70s. This prompted a large group of us to take up Taekwondo as our violent encounters were rapidly on the increase. Most of us only stayed to learn the art of self-defence and only one of our gang stayed on to accomplish becoming a black belt. This made us a streamlined fighting cell; we would take on all comers. We had a reputation for a good punch up and didn't really lose many. Some of our battles were pre-arranged and would take place in parks or sports fields before going to the pub. This gave a true account of all involved. No weapons just boots and knuckles.

The Towns had a large amount of armed forces stationed there, namely the Army and the Navy. None of us locals really liked them as they were always chasing after the local talent (girls). Thursday and Friday nights were always lively. We would use them as practice nights for a fight Squaddie and Matelot bashing. We would play up until the white caps put in an appearance (Military Police). They would fly down the road in open top jeeps, white helmets on their heads and baseball bat style batons as weapons. That was our usually our cue to leave!

Another top spot for a good old punch up was when the traveling fairground would visit. We would hang around the main attractions as they always played the music we wanted to hear. All it would take was a few faces to appear that we'd already had sport with and it would just go off like a firework display. Happy days they were!

We had a spell through the 70's where we went through what I would call semi-suedehead and by that I mean we would wear the Prince of Wales and Rupert check trousers and shoes that we called Toppers but we didn't do the hair thing. Toppers were an interesting item of footwear. They had crepe souls and were generally two colours (I had burgundy and black). They were worn quite often by Noddy Holder of Slade. They were just as comfortable as a well-worn pair of Doc Martens and actually looked the part as well.

By this time the scooters had all fallen by the wayside and we'd built up a small fleet of Anglia's, MK1 Cortina's and a Morris 1000. We could now travel in comfort and our clobber could stay as sharp as a knife. This led to us Medway lot getting into aggro with towns all over Kent: Maidstone, Sittingbourne, Margate, Ramsgate- to name but a few. Bank holiday weekends would mean Southend, Brighton, Hastings and, of course, Margate.

There was a bit of a skinhead revival late 70's/early 80's along with the two tone outbreak. I liked the music but didn't really like the new skinhead look that consisted of drain-pipe jeans, 10/14 hole Doc Martens, T shirts and braces dangling down. I'm sure it was this look that attracted people like the Nazi party and National Front and the like. Sadly anyone that dressed in the skinhead style would instantly get tarred with that brush and, believe it or not, we still do these days!

The 80s for me were very tame. I joined the same trend as many of my good friends. Got married to my lovely wife (Carol) and produced a lovely little girl (Leanne) and a chunky little boy (Rob). This really was full-on stuff. I had to work flat-out to pay the endless stream of bills (nothing's changed there then) but I would still make time to creep off out with the lads for a few beers.

Ska, Reggae and Rocksteady were always being played in my house and on the car stereo. My daughter Leanne grew to love it. She would get into my Granada and say "Put Smurf on, Daddy." I knew that she meant Double Barrel (Dave & Ansell Collins). She was convinced that they were singing "Smurf, Smurf, Smurf "during that song and that is what she would sing to it. I recently met Dave Barker and told him this story and he loved it. I left him with a real broad smile on his face.

We once took a family holiday at Dawlish in Devon (it must have been 25 years ago now). There was this bloke there that watched my every move. At the end of the week he finally came over and spoke to me, He said "Where do you get your clobber from? I used to wear all that stuff". That man was Danny Hatcher, one of the old G-Ranch skinheads from Maidstone. That prompted me to try and kick it all back off just as it used to be but without the violence.

This bright idea took literally years to put into effect but I finally managed to get a friend of mine, Andy, to lay on a Ska and Reggae night. Andy and his pal John had the sound system and I booked the venue, printed and sold the tickets. We shifted 60 tickets and eagerly awaited the night. It was absolutely spot-on. Some old and some new faces. What a night! Pressuredrop Sound System was born and Medway was back on the skinhead map! Pressuredrop was the only mobile Ska and Reggae sound system in the towns and it sure caused a stir!

I'm so pleased with the way the scene has picked up again with events going on every weekend. The Skinhead family just gets bigger and bigger with a helping hand from a little bit of social networking.

When my daughter Leanne reached the legal drinking age she started to come out to most of the Ska/Reggae events with me. In fact, she probably came to more events than my wife (who, incidentally, was a 70's Battersea Skinhead girl). Leanne had grown to love the music and the whole scene through growing up with it via my good self. She soon had a wardrobe full of tonic skirts, suits, shirts/blouses and very nice loafers. The feather cut hair topped it all off very nicely. We went all over the place for a good old dance with me laying on mini busses to make it all worthwhile.

Only one thing lets the scene down just a little and that is a hint of snobbery. Now don't get me wrong, I love the vintage clothing and I wear vintage clothing myself, but come on folks, it's not a photo shoot! Get on the dance floor and dance your vintage socks off. That's what it's always been about for me: Smart uniform, clothing buffed up, footwear whatever your choice and dancing to the music! It's sure to come to your town soon if it hasn't already and you never know -I might just be there!

144

GER'SNAKE HUGHES

It all started for me not long after I'd seen the film *Quadrophenia* in 1979. I was a Mod at the time and was in my last year at school. I loved Northern Soul at this point, my older brother also being a huge fan and a regular at Wigan Casino for the Northern Soul nights. Then along came Two Tone, which led me to rapidly become a skinhead. Many of my mates had also become skinheads here in Anglesey, North Wales, though a few were Punks. Brilliant times, and today at 50 years old I'm still polishing my Doc Martens and enjoying the scene. Proud and loud! I still attend as many scooter rallies as I possibly can, along with my family. Best scene by far!

Back in the 80s the skins would often get heavy law harassment. The police just didn't like us one bit, assuming we were all racist thugs. Think that stemmed from the media, as there were boneheads claiming to be "skinheads" (or, at least were labelled as such by the press) that were racist scum that we certainly would never associate with. Scum of the earth and complete no-hopers. If anything, it was a real insult to be seen by the law as being one of them. However, there was one brief period, all of us being raw 17-18 year-olds where some of us retaliated against this prejudice, basically playing up to the law's stereotypical view of all skinheads being racist. It was anger more than anything. We soon came to our senses though and realised that we were not doing the culture any favours, especially as our love of music was mostly of Jamaican origin. We learned from this and grew up and it's that brief period where we did almost become racist thugs that I regret, but we live and learn.

I can't think of a culture as strong as Skinhead. It's for life. I often say to my kids, "Do you think you'll still be listening to the same genre of music as you are now in thirty years' time?" I don't think so! I feel very lucky to still be on the scene enjoying it all. And the music: Northern Soul, Ska, Rocksteady and Reggae. Only a few of us remain now from the old days but so many still on the scooter rallies keeping the spirit alive.

Long may it continue! SKINHEAD CULTURE...THE BEST CULTURE!

SKINHEAD 1968:

I became a skinhead around 1969 when I was 15. Many other lads were too. As me and my mates all had our heads shaved, we weren't allowed to go on any school trips. None of our parents had much money, so there wasn't any spare cash for clothes. We used to wear second hand clothes, jeans with bottoms rolled up, original granddad vest, original wide braces, pit boots, black beret and army great coat which was green with brass buttons. These were non-branded clothes.

We then started to have a parting shaved into our hair. The hair was shaved with no guard so it was the shortest setting. It wasn't long after this that I left school. I was 15. Straight away I went into work, becoming an apprentice tool maker; the wage was about £2.50 a week. This enabled me to buy myself new clothes. I bought olive green Levis Sta-Prest, Ben Sherman checked shirt, tank top, black Harrington lined with red tartan and black Doctor Martins 8 holes. Cherry red docs weren't out yet so I had to go to Leicester to buy these clothes because it was the only stockists of this fashion. I later brought 16 hole cherry red docs and my girlfriend brought me a Crombie with red pocket handkerchief (3 points). I brought a black stingy brim pork pie hat, which had a very slim brim, not much at the front, and it was 5 inches high, and had a black wide band round with a bow at the back.

Gangs of us skinheads used to meet in the week and we'd usually stay local, then at weekends we used to meet in Belper and go to the Derwent Social Club.

On Saturday's we used to meet and go to watch the Rams play in Derby (sometimes we went on a Wednesday night). We travelled on the train from Ambergate. It was while we waited at the station at Derby for the away fans where it would all kick off. The mounted police would just ride into you to break up the fights. When we went to home matches at Derby we would try and climb into the Osmaston end but police dogs would mostly have us before we got in. One time we hid and waited behind a wall and then stoned the lot of them. One Saturday after the match a skinhead was knocked down by a car. A woman was driving and she had two small children in the back. The skinheads trashed her car. They smashed the window screen and jumped all over it. She was screaming, the kids were crying and were terrified but no one helped. They didn't hurt her or the children, just trashed the car. The city centre was mayhem at times; hundreds of skinheads fighting and nicking from shops.

On Sundays we used to wait on the railway bridge at Ambergate for the Hells Angels to ride through and then we would stone them, too. I remember one weekend where we had a big meet at Ambergate and we decided to wait for the Hells Angels. Once we saw them, we leapt at them, dragging each of them off their bikes. This made all the traffic come to a standstill on the A6! We used to carry flick knifes, cut throat razors and knuckle dusters. We'd sharpen the edges of pennies so we could throw them at the away fans; most of these weapons were for football violence. Razor blades were sewn into the lapels of our Crombies in case anyone grabbed you. I sometimes carried a machete which I kept in a leather sheath attached to my belt.

In the early days if you wore pit boots to the match, they would make you take them off. So to prevent this, our girlfriends used to hide our weapons in their boots in case we were searched, as obviously they never searched the girls. Our trick was when we went into the football ground one of us would pay and your mate would crawl through your legs as you went through the turnstiles. It was a way of saving what little money we had. It was the same on the trains as we would hide in the toilets throughout the whole journey to avoid paying. Other ways of getting our hands on money was in pubs where we would go in and take the collection tins off the bars. We'd go in the chippy and run off without paying.

Fights were constant; everywhere we went it would kick off, police would arrive and if you were unlucky to get caught you'd spend the night in a cell. It all added to the buzz and was like an adrenaline rush. At weekends, at local discos and pubs. One time they refused to serve us, so one of the lads took it upon himself to set fire to the back of the pub. Always remember another time the whole of the street was shut off; all skins were fighting with police.

Without going on forever, I have seen a lad get killed in a gang fight in Derby. He was stabbed, many others injured with different weapons. If you couldn't fight you had to learn to fight. A lot of the lads took up boxing. When on holiday during the second night there, my mate got his jaw broke; the violence just never stopped.

The life of a skinhead at this time was hard because you were always a target for police, buses wouldn't stop for you, jobs were hard to get. People felt threatened by us: even to this day when you go out dressed as a skinhead people still think you are out for trouble.

HENRY RUTHERFORD

I became a skinhead in the early 1980's, with a liking for the 2-Tone bands such as The Specials, The Beat, Bad Manners & Madness, and a lifelong loving of old Jamaican ska too, thanks to my father's influence.

To me, being a skinhead means music, friends and beer, and having that feeling of unity among many other like-minded folk, regardless of whether you've ever met before or not.

With thanks to Facebook, the social side of the scene is continuously increasing, thanks to pages/groups like Ska & Skins international, & Skinhead, Oi & Trojan tattoos.

Some of my most memorable moments are probably being on stage, singing along to 'Hurt so Good' with Susan Cadogan,& sitting on Dave Wakeling's tour-bus, after an English Beat gig in 2014, just a couple of my favourite artists, along with others like Nick Welsh (aka King Hammond),John Holt, Toots & The Maytals, Dandy Livingstone, Prince Buster,& Jimmy Cliff.

The only bad experiences for me is when others assume you have the same views as the more narrow-minded folk that like to try & hide themselves & their hatred amongst the scene.

PETE GRIFFIN

I was a skinhead at 11 then by 16 I got a Vespa 50 and moved to the mod scene for a long time, because of all the racism and I felt the Union jack was used for that purpose. I was never into Oi!, just the 2 Tone stuff, then the reggae, ska and northern soul. I remember hearing Prince Buster's 'One Step

Beyond', when me and my brother were getting ready for school and it freaked us out in a good way, found the single and got them to play both sides at the school disco, it went over the heads of all the other kids, haha.

We used to get the home boys come down to the discos. A few were skinheads, one black skinhead had a Union Jack t-shirt with 'I don't care I'm British' on it, a white rude boy kid use to walk around with a walking stick: he looked the part, Fred Perry black trousers, white socks and loafers. Never really had any fights, always had shit off bikers in the different villages, as there wasn't really many skinheads around Wrexham, Chester area, it was more the skinhead scooter boy look and, being up north, a lot of them were into soul music.

When I moved to the big school at eleven there were quite a few skinheads in the first year and they were listening to Madness, Specials etc and that's how I got into it, oh shit plus my best mates older brother had a Lambretta and his mates had scooters too, but they were all big fans of The Jam and about 8 or 9 years older than us. So different up here than the London thing. Seems to be a lot of Oi! and the white power stuff down London area with politics, I never did politics, never voted, just loved the music, having a dance and a few drinks, life is too short. I'm having the best time now, I fly the Union Jack with pride and I don't care what people think. If they think I'm racist, fuck 'em, I ain't. Lol.

CAI ROBERTS. 6 YR OLD SKINHEAD, SCOOTERIST, PRESTATYN, NORTH WALES

Cai has been a skinhead for about 4 years. He first asked for his hair to be cut, asking if he could be "bald like Granddad". He has always had a love for ska music. His favourite bands are Madness, The Specials, Bad Manners, and The Selector. He also likes some punk like Evil Conduct, Sham 69 and the Ramones.

Cal is an extravert: he oozes confidence and will chat to everyone. His love of scooters, too. He likes nothing than to jump on a Vespa and pretend he is travelling 60 MPH to a rally. He does go pillion on a few occasions and has done since he was 3 years old.

We as a family have always liked the scooterist/skinhead scene and went to the rallies back in the 80's which were manic and wouldn't dream of taking our daughter to them back then, even though, like Cai, she loved getting on the back of a scooter and going for a ride. Nowadays the scene is a little calmer and Cai attends the rallies as much as he can. He loves meeting up with all his skinhead friends who are mainly in their late 40's. He really does think he is one of the lads.

In 2013, we took Cai to his first to his first rally and music festival, where he surprised us all and got up on stage and started skanking with the band 2 Rude and singing 'Geno' on the microphone. He also got to meet the Lambrettas.

In 2013, we went to see Madness at Haydock Park, and being the extravert he is, he shouted 'Johnny Vegas'. Johnny Vegas loved Cai and practically spent the whole evening with him. He then took Cai on stage with him to dance to the finale and say goodnight to a crowd of 20,000 people. Johnny keeps up to date with what Cai is up to on Twitter and if you were to ever ask Cai who is his best friend, his reply will always be 'Johnny Vegas'.

We were approached by Dr Martens in 2013 and Cai was asked to appear in the cast for their AW14 campaign. As it was a long way to go to Covent Garden, they Skyped him and a few weeks later we received the news he had got the job. They travelled to Rhyl and did the photo shoot with Cai at the Rhyl scooter weekender in September 2013. The campaign went global and was in the shops from August 2014 to February 2015.

He has appeared in Scootering Magazine, a few times in the Modfather Advert with photos that John Card took at a rally.

In 2015, Gavin Martin asked for junior mascots for the Madness Grandslam Programme. I messaged him, but, unfortunately, had missed the deadline. He messaged me back a day later saying he would gladly fit him on the mascots page. Cai was thrilled, as Madness is his favourite band.

In July 2015, we went to Haydock Park to see Madness. Woody Woodgate had arranged for Cai to meet the band. Woody introduced Cai to the band as "this lad is more famous than us". He then had them all laughing and doing the Madness walk. He was then asked yet again to dance the finale and say goodnight.

Cai has danced with lots of bands and feels comfortable on stage dancing. It's where he wants to be most of all. He has had videos that have gone viral. He has met Madness, Lee Thompson Ska Orchestra, Neville Staple, Christine Staple, Roddy Byers, Buster Bloodvessel, Doug Sanders, Johnny Vegas, and Spencer Wilding. Some keep up to date with what Cai is doing.

Cai is currently in a film called *Womble the Movie*. He plays the character of Scooterboy, alongside Johnny Vegas,

Jimmy Cricket, Lee Thompson Ska Orchestra and Briana Corigan. The film will be released in 2016.

Cai is probably one of the most well-known little skinheads of today and loves to chat to all the people he meets and is well-known by most of the ska bands.

On the subject of Cai's granddad, Oliver, he has been a skinhead scooterist all his life. As for myself (nanny to Cai) I'm not a skinhead, though have always been into the skinhead/scooter scene, especially the music. Cai seems to be into it even more than we were, as he can't wait to put on his DM's and skank to the music. Neither of us are dancers, he has just picked it up himself. The way he dresses, he chooses himself. He prefers the Ben Sherman shirts but likes the Fred Perry polo. If it's a day event, he likes his Ma1 flight jacket but if it's an evening, likes to wear his Crombie or Harrington.

We have in the past had a lot of criticism from people for the way Cai is dressed, with comments like "his parents will be off drunk in the corner letting him run riot flicking the v's" etc. He is nothing like that. Yes he knows what swear words are and flicking the v's and the finger, but he also knows that it's wrong. He is in an adult world but kids these days learn most of that on a playground. I'm just glad he gets to go out, meet people, and enjoy the music and learn life skills rather than sit in front of a TV learning how to shoot at things.

Personally I don't drink, and I know that people that meet Cai usually love him and think he is just like any other 6 year old kid-- a little cheeky, with a lot of confidence, a little character, loving the scene and is part of the next generation of skinhead scooterists - and a special one at that.

CHRIS CARRINGTON

 It was around 1979-1980 that I became a skinhead, thanks to the 2 Tone ska revival. The reason for this was my love of the music and the clothes.

Being a skinhead then was to me all about looking good and being with mates who felt the same, whether it be at the football, a night on the town or a bank holiday away. There was always a sense of being a part of something, whatever that was--band of brothers maybe.

Being a skinhead now still holds the same values to me as it did back then, although with some it seems to be a lot more about what you wear - suits ,shirts etc. In my case, not much has changed in what I wear as it's almost the same as what I wore back in the early eighties, although I never went in for jeans up by your knees and never wear more than eight hole boots. So it's about pride in the way you look and, of course, the music and being a traditional skin it has to be reggae and soul for me, plus a bit of 70's punk and glam rock-- all this thrown together to me gives a feeling of again being a part of something different to normal day to day life of most people.

I think my most memorable time being a skin was on a scooter run to Great Yarmouth and getting to see Desmond Dekker live on stage. The place was electric, but it also holds one of the worst memories for me as NF skins stormed the stage and we had to fight our way out.

Violence was part and parcel of being a skinhead back in the day, whether at football or bank holidays or scooter rallies, even in town fighting between estates and schools, so it was sort of part of the norm. Thankfully we are all now too old to be bothered with that aggro now and the scene today seems more vibrant with even old enemies' now firm friends.

Racist skins or boneheads featured a lot in the eighties and there seemed to be a split. Some of us going back to the roots with the music and clothes, hard, sharp and smart, and others going towards the white noise, jeans up to arse daubed in Nazi regalia brigade. These types I had no time for and still don't. In the eighties I was part of the sharp movement in the South- West, which brought me into conflict with NF, BM and c18 boneheads and also on many scooter rallies we had many run ins with them. Sadly, there are still many about who like to voice their opinions on many skin sites on the web and Facebook. However, like back in the day, those who were/are us know what it is about and keep the faith!

SEAN MARSHALL

Becoming a skinhead was a sort of natural progression from being a Mod. From around 1982 I became more aware of ska, reggae & rocksteady and delved into the material that the 2 Tone lot were covering - the likes of Desmond Dekker, Prince Buster, Bob Marley & the Wailers, Skatalites etc. I guess I preferred the raw, more rhythmic sounds of reggae/ska etc. to the 60's mod/R&B sounds, although I still like that genre of music, as well as soul.

Being a skinhead is all about pride in one's looks and appearance, having proper ethics about life's choices, i.e. look after family & friends, work hard, earn a living, provide for family and live a full and happy life without strife and worry - Oh, and having a few nights out with the missus at a reggae do with friends, either participating or providing, as

I've been a DJ of ska/reggae for 3 years now and it's a massive part of my passion. I love the music and thrive on the culture from where it heralded from: Jamaica. It's clichéd I know, but it's like being part of a "family", the camaraderie is second to none. I guess the Northern Soul scene may be similar. Travelling to skinhead reggae events up and down the country (Glasgow, Dundee, Edinburgh, Bristol, Manchester, Birmingham, Halifax, Oxford, Southend and Margate) gives me and my missus a chance to meet up with great friends - you'd have to be there to get the gist of what I mean.

The most memorable events would have to be the Margate & Southend skinhead reggae weekends. We never miss the yearly gigs and have met some fantastic skinheads and skingirls - also my first ever shot at DJ'ing at Pressure Drop in Middlesbrough, courtesy of the event organiser, Paddy Muldowney - because of that intro into that side of being a skinhead it prompted me to create Gateshead Reggae Club, which is in its second year. I don't really have any bad memories as such, other than missing out on Skagate (Margate's skinhead gig) last year 'cos we were skint - B&B costs, travelling expenses and accommodation are well expensive from up North where we live, Newcastle upon Tyne. That's possibly down to me buying too many records and skinting us ... oops!

I can honestly say, hand on heart I have never came across any violence because of the life I've chosen - yeah, I get a few comments from folk saying, "Oh, I used to be a skinhead" - lots of our mates say they've encountered this before, but as far as I'm concerned, once a skinhead , always a skinhead. I mean, why the fuck would you become something to give it up and for why? Seems a tad shallow for my liking. I've come to the conclusion that skinheads aren't seen as often as they used to, as in they're not as revered or feared any more - you don't see many "bootboy", bleachers, 14i Doc Martens, pilot jacket-wearing Nazi-boys anymore, although they definitely still do exist. I'm definitely not into that 79/80's Oi! scene in the slightest - I prefer the Trad '69 onwards, skinhead thesis and ideals, especially towards the threads AND the music.

We were once at a SLF tribute bands' gig (I know the lead singer and thought we'd pop along for support) when a mini-bus load of said 80's style bootboys turned up and started sieg heiling and all that mouthy shit - made for a very uncomfortable atmosphere. They're from a neighbouring city and we're not associated with them at all!

It's rumoured that some of them MAY have been responsible for an attack on my mate's missus, who is Jamaican and they've been together for years - he's Scottish by the way and one of the other 2 members of Gateshead Reggae Club (sorry for plugging our club, ha ha ha). Also, one time when we were doing a gig in my mates' local there was this random, pissed up trendy who was popping snide comments at his missus for being black. He wasn't a skinhead but it might emphasise that racism rears its ugly head in all walks of life - the lad got a barring from the Manager and, I suspect, a good hiding at a later date off my mate Scotch Kev, my fellow DJ, ha ha.

JOHN QUELCH

I was first introduced to the culture of skinhead by my best friend Rod. We had become friends from an early age (about 5 years old). Rod had moved from London with his family to Wooburn Bucks, a village about 25 miles west of London. Rod had visited family back in the capital where Skinhead had become a major thing in 1970. When I heard what he had experienced, we both then decided we had to be a part of this.

As we were both from working class families we felt that it was a natural way of life. We both worked and saved hard so we could buy the clothes, i.e. DM's, Levi jeans, Ben Sherman or Brutus, braces etc. Six months on we had grown to about twelve of us and called ourselves WOOBO SKINS, taking the name WOOBO from the name of our village Wooburn Green. Being a Skinhead was having pride in yourself and your friends, to watch each other's' backs and always stick together. Jamaican music was a must--old ska i.e. Prince Buster, Toots, Upsetters and many more. Even though this was 40 years ago, the next generations of young people of the village still use our name WOOBO as a nickname for the village, which still makes us smile. We did have quite a few fights with motorcycle gangs back then: they were our main rivals as we had a completely different way of life.

But, to be honest, football became our main outlet for fighting. Tottenham was our team. We would go to home and away games, saw some scary shit back then. Looking back, we were lucky to have survived that! I honestly think Skinheads being racist are a bit of a myth, back then we had lots of coloured friends. The music brought us together, going to clubs and dancing to ska and reggae together; great times.

We still talk about it now when the subject crops up. I'm 57 now and still wear the Harrington, Crombie, etc, tell stories to the kids about how it was back then, they love it, but the main message we put over to them is have pride in yourself and where you come from, never back down to anyone. Skinhead is a way of life, working class people having pride in themselves. The saying is true of Skinhead culture; if you were a part of it back then you were in the middle of something special, if you wasn't, you wouldn't understand.

JAKE JONES

I initially became a skinhead because of a friend. I was receiving a lot of bullying as a kid and he just basically took my mind off all of that by getting me into the music and the clothes. When I left school I got into it a lot more and it helped me find the person I am today

Being a skinhead to me has always been about the music, culture, drinking and belonging to something where you're accepted and loved instantly by many generations and from people from all walks of life. It has never been about racism or political views. I know I have always been a skinhead, not because I have to, because I love it.

Around 2014 I went away to get recovery in a rehabilitation unit. There were so-called friends I didn't even hear from unless they wanted a favour. My skinhead friends, however, were always there. I was always getting letters and phone calls, even from a skinhead who had never met me before was giving me encouragement and support.

When I first started out on the scene I earned my place with a skinhead gang called The 13th Lucky Skins, which no true skinheads were a part of, just bald heads with a pair of Dr Martens looking to get fucked and start trouble. We used to meet with other groups of people and fight for a hat of drugs and money. But it didn't last long and everyone parted, leaving me feeling like the only true skinhead left.

When some people want to become a skinhead they think it's all about fighting, drinking and protecting your country but I think that is bollocks. Obviously you choose your own story by your actions but I find the older skinheads look after me and keep me out of trouble, which in turn makes me want to teach new skinheads what it's really about and how to follow the right path.

People are quite quick to judge and instantly think you're part of a racist sub group such as EDL and others sometimes walk up to me and ask me questions or sing parts of ska songs as I walk by, so the reviews are, to say the lease, quite mixed.

I can honestly say I have never met a racist skinhead—it's never been about race or political views so it does hurt me when people assume that you're a racist, because you are far from it. I have only ever met one true racist bonehead whose views were only ever about race and never about skinhead culture. So in my eyes he was a racist, which has no connection to being a skinhead, he was just bald and thought he was a skinhead. There are skinheads and boneheads. Boneheads have no connection with skinheads, they just happen to have a 'skin-head' and claim to be a skinhead, but the good thing is that no original skinhead would even go near him/her, let alone share the same views.

JASON HUGHES

I was born October 1969 in Reading, Berkshire. I became a skinhead as a child in 1977. From birth, reggae was drummed into me as my parents loved it. They used to go to house parties with their black friends, and as a child I was always playing about with my black friends and their parents always played reggae and fed me on curries and chicken. Then I saw some skins, and thought I liked that look. My friend's dad had a barber's on Southampton St, Reading and I asked him to shave all my hair off.

When I got home my mum lost the plot! But I was adamant that's what I wanted. But later on I got beaten up when I went to see some friends from another part of Reading, one time being from a skinhead because I was with a couple of black friends. I later found out that these skins hated blacks, and then I got into a fight for being a skinhead by a gang of black kids for being a skinhead, so I changed. Then, in 1979, I heard the Specials on the radio, I was hooked! I remember I was the only kid in school wearing a Crombie and pork pie hat. Finally I was happy again and I could do what I wanted without looking over my shoulder.

In my last year at collage I started DJing with some friends and even though I had hundreds of reggae records, I started doing everyday pub gigs. Personally I hated it, but it was what it was. After my separation from my first wife in 1999 I had all my gear and records stolen, thousands of them, and then in 2004 I realised I was still a skinhead at heart. In October 2005 I started Dj'ing again, but this time only reggae and this has since become a regular event called DO THE SKA. Now I have found myself with a skinhead girl to be my wife and I know now I will die a skinhead.

LIZZ HANDLEY

I became a skinhead in 2012, at the age of 13, after watching a few films and seeing a few skinheads around where I live. I decided to look further into the scene. With my boyfriend at the time being into the scene as well it was all great. The first was mainly just thinking I was cool walking around in unpolished Doc's and a Harrington. After being in the scene a few months, my fashion changed completely and it went from just a pair of Docs and a Harrington to a full wardrobe of shirts, polos, Harringtons, sheepskins, tonic skirts, bleachers...everything I wore was somehow related to the fashion of skinheads.

In the summer of 2013, now at the age of 14, I told my friends I wanted a feather cut and-- friends being friends-- they dared me to. They even booked the appointment for me. Walking to the hairdressers, I now understood that I was eventually going to take a big leap and join the scene properly. The hairdressers didn't even know where to start, but 2 hours later after my curly locks had been cut and shaven off I had eventually gotten my well-deserved feather cut. I was over the moon at the fact I had now gone the whole way and gotten the skinhead girl haircut. Believe it or not, it cost £15 and has to be the best £15 I've ever spent.

Being a skinhead to me means independence as I'm the girl that stands out from all the other girls. I'm the person that has always stood out, but until finding the skinhead scene, never really knew how to. But it also means my identity: I couldn't imagine myself without a feather cut, fishnets and Doctor Marten boots. The skinhead subculture has really become a homely community for me, and somewhere I feel accepted, after so many years of struggling to find my place I find the skinhead scene is my home. Putting on my fishnets and Crombie has got to be the best thing out there.

I have quite a few good and bad memories of being a skinhead, whether being chased through Wolves because of dressing like a skinhead, to being escorted to my 'prom' by a load of scooters whilst wearing my tonic suit. The scene really has impacted on my life and I wouldn't change my appearance for anyone. Don't get me wrong, I've been turned down at jobs because of my appearance not being 'professional' enough and I also had a lot of trouble at school for looking the way I did. When the headmaster told me I wasn't allowed my hair past a certain length, what did I do? I had it cut a hell of a lot shorter....But I've also had some ace times as well: my 16th birthday party was in the pub where my scooter club - Telford Saints Scooter Club - meet, I had my friends Sarah and Tim from Simmer Down DJ for me, and it had to be the best night of my life! I enjoyed it so much, I even invited a couple of my friends down to see what the scene was like and why I love it so much. I even got my best friend, Emily, up on the dance floor dancing to 'Skinhead Moonstomp.' I guess the best memory I have although isn't as skinhead related--it is finally getting my scooter on the road, which my dad and boyfriend helped me with. After two years of restoring my scooter, I finally got on the road this year and it has got to have been one of the best experiences of my life.

The only violence I have been involved in as a skinhead was during school when a girl that kept calling me names because of my hair upset me that much I decided to give her a good hiding as my dad told me to. This girl couldn't even fight back, she tried pulling my hair but I didn't have much to pull. I never got bullied after this...I guess in a way, I succeeded.

In regards to any conflict with racist skinheads, I wouldn't say yes but then I wouldn't say no. I'm not the sort of skinhead that would name myself as either left or right wing. If I'm totally honest, I don't really think much about politics at the age of 16. I have friends that are SHARP's and I have friends who are right wing and support WPWW, but I personally-and I know that this is just matter of opinion-don't understand why we have to label ourselves as either this or that.

CAT LYONS

Basically, I was 11/12 years old when the second generation of skinhead erupted in the early 80s. I was living in Southend on Sea and every bank holiday tons of skinheads would get the train from London and invade our seafront. I loved it and would go down to see them all, so I guess that's where it started for me. I was too young to become one as such, but as I got older I got more into the scootering scene and was a rockabilly for a few years, but always loved how the skins looked and the music.

I took a break for a few years while I had my kids, then in the late 90s I started going back to rallies and ska gigs. The urge to be a skin was growing as time went on but I was a bit chicken about having my hair shaved off, lol. In the end I went for it and never looked back! I've immersed myself into the skin world now, and I wish I'd not waited so long.

We are like a big family and have each other's backs. There are some elements of being a skinhead I don't like, such as the politics, the skinhead/bonehead mix ups, the racism etc. Also the arguments as to where skinhead started, who is wearing the right stuff, how you're not proper 'cos your turn ups aren't right...in that respect you can be crucified. It's not for the faint hearted, lol. But, at the end of the day, we all get together and look great, dance to brilliant music and have a fabulous time. I don't see me ever changing from this now: I have finally found my little niche in the world.

CARL WOODY WHITNEY

 I became a skinhead in 1980 after I had moved into comp school. I had become interested in the look after seeing groups of older skinheads walking to school. By this time I had gotten into the 2 Tone era and was listening to the likes of Madness, the Specials, Bad Manners and the Beat and was also picking up on the skinhead/mod look that was everywhere in 1979/80.

As a result, I started to knock about with older lads and soon was part of a mob who ranged in age from 13 to early 20s, all of whom were from my local area. At that age I was looking up to the older lads. Most weekends we hung around outside a local amusement arcade known as the P.L.A and down what is known to locals as the embankment. This was a large area of parkland next to a river in the city centre.

We also used to mob up and go into the local indoor shopping complex around 82/83 but was always moved on by security guards who knew we could be trouble. By 82 I was into Oi!. I had already been listening to bands like Sham69, so was already liking the sound, and then my favourite bands were the likes of 4skins, Blitz, Cockney Rejects, Infa Riot and Condemned 84, amongst others. Back then I wore mainly market Sta-Prest and 2nd hand jeans, which I rolled up to the length of me DMs. I bought market Harringtons and normally cheaper button-downs with no particular names as long as they looked ok. I did own a few Ben Shermans that I had bought me for Xmas or birthdays and I did pinch a few from shops.

I got into a lot of trouble during my teenage years and was in and out of the local nick, but mainly for petty crimes: theft, joy riding scooters and anti-social activities-- say no more. After being thrown out of school at 14, I was sent to a local detention centre called Fletton detention centre (is still there I believe) between 8am-4pm to complete the last year. Basically to keep us off the streets!

By 1985 I was in trouble again and was sent to court but was saved from borstal after being given one more chance by a retired local policeman who saw some potential in me. He put me into a boxing class situated above a pub where I went for a few years, which was more anger management really. I got a job through a friend of a friend of a friend!! This was at a local frozen food place around 86/87. By that time I was calming down and earning money.

I had started to listen to Trojan more than the Oi! and was slowly getting into more of the 60s ska and reggae. By 1992 though, I had a very steady girlfriend and was drifting away from the skinhead way of life, as there seemed less and less of us and had gone stale around Peterborough. It never went away from me heart and I never got into anything else, my hair remained fairly short if not a little wild for a year or so.

By 95/96 I was back into it ... to me it never went away. I just am not me without me button down shirt and braces, Levis or wranglers and me cherry reds!! Over the last 16 years or so, I've really got into the 69 era more and more, thanks to mates I've met and attend dos/events all over the country when I can. It's about being smart, having a sense of pride in yourself and the music!!

STEVE ROWORTH

 I first became a skinhead, aged 9, in 1969. It was in the school summer holidays. I was walking through my local estate when I saw 3 skinheads who were probably in their late teens. They looked really smart and hard. I always remember thinking to myself 'please don't beat me up'. The next day I nicked some money out my mom's purse and took myself to a barbers, and asked for a skinhead cut. He asked, 'Does your mom know?' I replied 'She gave me the money', so he cut my hair. When I got home she went berserk. When my dad got home from work he thought it was funny, and he took me to get some monkey boots that weekend. Can't remember how long it lasted.

I became a skinhead again in the late seventies when I was working and could buy my own clothes. It felt really good being able to get my Dr Martens and Crombie on the same day. I used to drive my mom crazy asking to turn my Wranglers up. I got back into it again about 3 years ago, and have made some of the best mates in this time. It was a chance meeting with Chris Carrington and Johnny Mac at a local northern soul, reggae and Motown night that started it off again, and not looked back since. I go to events now from Brighton to Birmingham, Tamworth, Walsall and Sunderland. No politics, just old and new skins having a good time.

I've had a couple of fights as a skinhead but only because of twats taking the piss of how we dress. With regards to the racist skinheads, they tried to get me into the NF down the football but I never got into it, as they say it's about the music and friendship, not the colour of the skin. After all, most of the music is black. I like the old original ska the best, with the likes of Toots and The Maytels, Laurel Aitken and

Symarip. I also like the Specials and the Beat. I don't mind a bit of modern-ish stuff like Cock Sparrer, Argy Bargy, the Last Resort, Combat 84, and a local band 'No Quarter'. As clothes, I still love wearing my Brutus shirts or Fred Perry polos with Sta-Prest or Levis 501 with docs or loafers. Love my mal, but must say, can't beat wearing a Crombie.

FRANK CASTLE

It was the summer of 1990, I was 14, and a few Punk-rockers I knew invited me to come with them to a party. There were Skins present and I just instantly knew that I wanted to be one. In the beginning, I wasn't much more than a bald thug, but I stuck with it and evolved.

To me, being a Skinhead means being straight up awesome. In all seriousness, I associate it with looks, music, patriotism and tough guy attitude, usually working class background, but I reject the notion that someone from a different background can't be just as much into it, not to mention that many of us raise their status later in life, by getting promotions, etc.

One very memorable experience was getting punched in the ribs by Wattie Buchan! Another was putting an end to my gay-basher days, when a Skin brother came out and some of us wanted to smash him up, whilst others took his side. I chose to be one of the latter. I only ever did that crap because back then because being called gay was not something a teenage boy wanted. After that day I no longer cared, and decided to be openly and vocally anti-homophobic.

In my younger days, I was into picking fights and seeking out trouble. Nowadays, I fight when I have to, that's it. Normally, I just ignore extremist knobheads and refuse to refer to them as Skinheads, be they far-right, far-left, or whatever, I've never done crap like SHARP either. But when they directly hassle or attack someone because of their skin colour, religion or sexual orientation, then I feel that it's my duty to intervene, but that's more me personally than the fact that I'm a Skin. One could argue that I used to be a violent Islamophobe after 9/11, and that it took me a while to snap out of that, but that had nothing to do with being a Skin, that was me personally being emotionally fucked up. Other than that, I prefer to not give them the time of day, unless they say or do something that stupid that I can't help extensively taking the piss out of them!

I find it very hard to name clear favourites, there are so many great musicians, but the most significant influences on me most certainly are The Maytals, Desmond Dekker, Laurel Aitken, Bob Marley, Cockney Rejects, Sham 69, The Exploited, Sex Pistols, Percy Sledge, and even some stuff outside the 'official' Skinhead range, sometimes just one or two songs, sometimes an entire band, and three entire genres. My favourite clothing are: Harringtons, sheepskin coats, denim jackets, Fred Perry polos, Ben Sherman button-downs, Union Jack and Trojan t-shirts, braces, Levi's 501 and burgundy Underground "Ranger" boots with long, round, white laces. I also wear an additional belt, just for a Union Jack buckle.

ROB EDDOLS

I became a skinhead in 1969. Lad next door was older and a mod. Followed the fashions and music, noticed in about 68 the hair was getting shorter. At 16 I bought a Lambretta and used to go to Bristol Locarno. All the fashions were becoming evident and the music shifted from Stax/Atlantic/Motown to incorporate Bluebeat and Trojan.

My hair became chopped to 1/16 inch, razored in parting and sideburns were cultivated. The reaction of parents and family to my new look was basically one of gobsmacked disgust. My uncle refused to speak to me as I obviously was one of those who 'fought with the police'.

Being a skinhead gave me an identity and meant that I belonged to a new, exciting, vibrant scene. Music and fashions were what it was all about, as well as the dangerous undercurrent that was all too evident. Football was high on the agenda. As part of Bristol City's East End Bootboy mob, there was always going to be trouble.

My dilemma is that the skins I knew from town were all Rovers Tote End Boys. So when we played each other I had to take a back seat when it came on top.

Most memorable moment was at Bristol Top Rank, watching Desmond Dekker and the Aces. Was upstairs in awe of the sea of bald heads bobbing up and down on the packed dance floor, that moment will live with me for ever.

Amusing incident at same venue with mystery band, revolving stage turned round to reveal Sweet, complete with long hair and an audience of gobsmacked skinheads who weren't exactly chuffed with their presence.

Violence- had a few rows with other skinheads in town. Best ones were at football. Crowds weren't segregated and "end-taking" was the name of the game.

August 1970 saw City play Sunderland at home. They had just been relegated from the old First Division and had arrived early and took up residence in the middle of our end. They had left "artwork" on walls outside proudly proclaiming that "Fulwell End" were in attendance.

Our mob came in, shouting "Sunderland". Sunderland's mob started cheering, thinking their numbers were being further swelled. 50 feet away the chant changed to "BRRRRIISSSTOLLL". We went steaming into them, DM's flashing at them. Plod got between us. Each time we scored, they charged us and vice-versa. There I was, in hitched up Levis, orange T Shirt, red braces and DM's. A copper was looking intensely at me and on the next charge he put me in a headlock, whilst his mate proceeded to beat me with his truncheon. My back, arse and legs were all treated to a flurry of blows. At the back of the end, he threw me down the step, picked me up and slammed me against the wall. "Right you little cunt, what are you gonna do about this?" My feet were off the floor as he held my throat. Thankfully he just threw me out. One consolation is that I am now 62. The copper was about 35, so he's now either dead or incontinent.

My main worry was that the match was on Match of the Day and I was shitting myself that Mum and Dad would see me in action.

Racist skinheads were mainly an 80's phenomena. The second wave skinheads were more extreme in every respect. We were brought up on Jamaican culture and music. There weren't many Asians in those days. I've come into contact with 80's skins at scooter rallies. All into Oi! and a bunch of Nazis that I have no time for. Imposters who hijacked the image and gave us all a bad press.

JAMES J ALLEN

Never been a skinhead. Closest I've been to being one is a suedehead which evolved from the skinhead subculture. Being a suedehead is about knowing where you come from. Keeping yourself grounded.

Good experiences is when walking down the road and people recognising me and paying me compliments. Bad experience is being called a sell-out because I have friends that are skinheads and people judging me on that. When people don't know the true meaning of the word 'skinhead' and making their own conclusions on it!

When the 80's so-called skinheads jumped on the bandwagon and caused conflict between blacks and whites, they were not there for the music, but to create havoc on the 2 Tone scene, in my opinion. People who I thought were friends at the time came out showing their true colours. Nothing I could do about it but keep my distance.

I came to blows with racist skins on several occasions growing up. I remember one time walking down the road with some mod mates in the west end and a bunch of boneheads came walking towards us, one of them being a bloke from near where I lived at the time. We didn't want trouble so we crossed the road to avoid them. They proceeded to cross over too, which was when we knew there was going to be trouble. Several of us had just purchased new jackets, shirts and Sta-Prest trousers from Carnaby street and knew we were gonna get them either dirtied or torn.

A fight broke out, blood splatters on the new threads, busted lips, black eyes and sore ribs. We got the better of them but by hell did it hurt!

Another time was at Charing Cross Station, mid 80's. I and a girl who I was seeing at the time got beaten up. I was black, she was white... you do the math! 3 quarter length bleached jeans, jack boots. I was no longer on the scene and turned more to soul music, so I wasn't dressed in ties and tonics. They just thought it would be funny!

My favourite artists are from the 60's. I would listen to them mostly because of my parents' record collection. Dennis Alcapone, The Maytals, Dave & Ansell, Desmond Dekker, Prince Buster, Laurel Aitken, Allton Ellis, Harry J, The Temptations, Bobby Womack... the list goes on.

I got into it more, so around the time of 2 Tone, I didn't really get into 2 tone but through it got to learn more about Caribbean music. My parents are not from Jamaica but from St Kitts and Montserrat in the West Indies, so the music was slightly different, but nevertheless brought up on ska, rocksteady and early reggae. Also on Motown!

DAVE RUMSEY (Toast)

 It started with Two Tone (I actually became a rude boy before becoming a skinhead). Me and a few mates were watching Top of the Pops, and the Specials came on with "Message to You Rudy". I was fifteen, with at the time on real identity, I used to skateboard and listen to a mixture of music, some rock like ACDC, Led Zeppelin, bit of punk like the Clash, Sham 69, Ruts, Bob Marley, just a mix really.

Our fashion was also a mix: Levi's, pumps a (converse type shoe). But I also had a Harrington as these were up the local market and all of us had one. We looked at what the band was wearing and we're almost wearing the same, it was affordable. I got my mum to get me a pair of ten hole DM's, I said they were for school, they were black. My hair up till then was long, so I got a French crop, which is probably more suedehead, but at the time I knew nothing of this. So as a group of friends we started to follow the music, some of our other friends were mods, but I never really liked the Jam, but Secret Affair were ok. Then a couple of lads in my class came in with skinhead haircuts, like some of the older boys a year above us.

I think it was a few months later that we went to Margate for Bank Holiday Monday, back then, every bank holiday Margate would be the place to go for a fight. The local firm were the Margate skins, they all used to wear Red Harrington's and fight anyone. Well, me and a couple of mates were walking along and a small group of the Margate skins saw us and shouted abuse and chased us into Dreamland. We did fucking run, and my mate said 'why we running? We are the same as them', well-apart from the hair, so we stopped. It turned out they thought we were mods. We got a bit of stick but I actually knew one of them. So we didn't get beaten up. We had a good laugh that day, although somewhat scary.

Back then it wasn't as clear cut as now, a skinhead was a skinhead, whatever politics he followed. We were kids out to shock and to have a laugh, I felt I should be a skinhead, so I slowly got my hair cut shorter each time: I sort of evolved into it. At the same time I looked more into the music, looking back to the early reggae, Trojan Reggae. I remember a mob of us at school had the logo painted onto the back of our Harrington's. At that time I didn't know about Blue beat, it was just Trojan Reggae.

I had a punk mate who knocked round with us and he went to school with a drummer in a new band called the Last Resort, it was through him I was introduced to Oi music. The Last Resort were from Herne Bay, Another band which influenced them to form were called the Rivals, they were a local punk band.

By now I was learning about other bands and about the Shop & The Last Resort. The hair got shorter. Every Bank Holiday I would be over Margate, joining other skins to have a row with the Mods and Soulies that turned up. By 1982, Two Tone had all but gone and I was listening to Oi!, I was visiting the Last Resort when I could, once or twice a year to pick up records and t-shirts.

Yes, like many I brought Skrewdriver releases, "All Skrewed UP" and "Back with a Bang", they were good. I was patriotic: I believed in my country, we had just won the Falkland war. But some of my mates got more into it and I could never really understand the Nazi side, I was working class, my granddad had escaped from Poland because of the Nazis, he was a pilot and helped in the battle of Britain. By then it had become Rock against Communism. Oi! had almost been killed off by Politics and it had soldiered on.

It was around 1982 I got my first scooter: a Vespa PX125, a friend had got a trail bike but I couldn't get the hang of the gears. A mod mate suggested a Scooter. I rode one and was hooked. A Ramsgate Skinhead called Skin rode a cut down Lambretta and some of my old school friends had scooters, so I became a scooter skin. Me and Steve went to Brighton as skinheads with our local mods, and they weren't too chuffed to see us, we got spat at and started on and ended up in a pub with a load of punks. But it was a great weekend, within a year scooter boys were appearing. A few of the Margate skins also had scooters, I seem to remember.

A few of my mates had now formed a skinhead band called Razor Sharp, the lead singer was a good friend, but had also become right wing, I followed the band locally but never went to see them when they played a RAC gig in Suffolk, after which they split. They were a good band and it was only really the singer who had the politics in his heart, to the others it was about the music.

Being working class, I supported the miners' strike and it was around now that I really got into politics. I had always been Labour as the Tories did nothing but fuck up the working classes. The local NF that my mates were involved in was just Tories in disguise. It was now I met a friend Ray (RIP) who was a huge influence on me. The night we met I was pissed up and we got into a tussle, I had seen him about and he was a Chelsea hooligan. But I stood my ground, it got broken up and the next day I saw him again, he came over to me and offered to get me a drink. As we chatted, he realised I wasn't right wing (back then, too many a skinhead was a Nazi).

It was him who introduced me to The Redskins, and I went to see them on a number of occasions. At one such Miners' benefit I met a few other skinheads who produced a fanzine called Stand Up and Spit. At the gig it all kicked off as some right wing causals had turned up. That's when I first saw Red Action, and, contrary to popular belief, there were Red Action Skinheads at that time. Ray went on to help form The Blaggers and, funny enough, the singer from Razor Sharp was asked to join No Remorse, which he turned down, and at this time we all used to drink together in the same pub. It was around 1986 that I started to hear about some new ska bands appearing in London. Link Records started and I started to collect their releases. I missed out on a few gigs as I was buying my first house. But in 1988 I made it to the Brixton academy, to see Laurel Aitken, Floyd Lloyd, the Potato 5, the Trojans and others. It was here I met some of my old Redskins mates and met George Marshall of Zoot and in December that year I was at the Brixton Fridge for Bad Manners, the Deltones, and Laurel Aitken.

Myself and my wife attended a lot of gigs and by the tail end of 1989 I had released my first issue of the Skinzine "Tighten Up". I had tried to model it on the sussed zine "Hard as Nails". I did "Tighten Up" until 1995. It featured Oi, ska and a little reggae, and it had little digs at the right wing scene, which I did not believe was skinhead by that time. The S.H.A.R.P movement started and at first it was a good idea, then it got into politics and now it has lost its impact.

In 1995 I got offered a job with One Stop Music, by Lol of Link music who I used to see at football. I ran the mail order department, until we handed it over to George who had now started "Pulped", after finishing the "Skinhead Times". I then ran a small Ska/ Reggae mail order called Ska Shack and worked for Moon Ska Europe for a while. At this time I started to DJ in London for a club called Sublime, which played Ska, Punk, Reggae, Ska-punk and a small amount of Oi! By now I was collecting Reggae and Ska on both cd and vinyl and trying to bring up my kids.

When Sublime shut, I felt I wanted to do a traditional Skinhead reggae night, a few of my friends from back in the day were back into it and so I started to put on reggae nights in Margate at the Westcoast bar, they weren't very successful but ok, One young lad asked if he could DJ with me and slowly a scene down here developed and we haven't looked back since. We got asked to spin tunes on an internet radio station and I still do. I started another paper fanzine called "Spirit Of 69" Skinzine, which does ok.

If you asked me when I was 16 about what being a skinhead means to me, it would have been about fighting, shagging girls and getting pissed, it was about belonging, smart clothes, and smart attitude, about honour.

Today it's about having a laugh, dressing smart, working class attitude, honour, music. In fact, not much has changed except I married the girl and I'm a little too old to fight. I think most Skinheads have the same values: respect, honour, and looking out for family and friends. When George Marshall asked me this in an interview for the TV program World of Skinheads, I think I rambled on about Skinheads being like the knights of old. But I was very, very drunk.

Some of the most memorable experiences include Margate 1984. There was only about 30 of us at the clock tower gardens and about 400 hundred Mods came across the beach, they came up to the gardens and one mod started on the local nutter, who hit the mod with a bit of a deck chair, we all ran forward and 400 odd mods ran back to the beach. That felt good until the old bill set the dogs on us.

Meeting Laurel Aitken and trying to interview him, I was so pissed my wife did it. Chatting to Prince Buster, having a curry with Rancid when I interviewed them for my first fanzine. Seeing the Skatalites in Berlin. The Last Resort playing Canterbury with the Elite, and it all kicked off-- had to walk home because we missed the train back.

Now, asking if a skinhead has been directly involved in violence is like asking Muhammad Ali if he boxes. Yes and I would think most skinheads have, back in the 80's there was always trouble. Some with other Skinheads, or other groups: Soul Boys, Greasers/Bikers, Mods, and sometimes Punks. From my own perspective, I don't think I started fights, but would always stand my ground. I never thought of myself as hard like some skinheads did, just average. I had my 50th this year and a mate I haven't seen for over 25 years turned up.

We spoke about the old times, and one of the things he said, he always thought of me as a lover not a fighter. So could never understand why I was always the first one in, as I was normally the first one to get decked. I lost more fights than I won, was hospitalized twice, one for a brain haemorrhage, and the other two soul boys attacked me while shopping for cakes with my girlfriend. The police came to the hospital to arrest me for criminal damage to the car the lads threw me into, my face hitting the door had caused 200 quid worth of damage. It was dropped.

I have used weapons, but never carried a knife, I did stab a mate in the stomach, but that was in my house, and was sort of an accident. Today those that haven't lived it will never understand the skinhead scene of the 80's. Punk and Oi! played an important part, as did politics. Some took it seriously: some just flirted with the right wing side of things.

I had always thought myself working class, so was always to the left, but at the same time I was proud to be English, proud of this land. My forefathers fought and died in the First World War, working class men, used as pawns by the upper classes gave their lives that made me proud. I wore a Union Jack t-shirt as did many others. Today many see that as racist because of the way it has been twisted. I could not understand why some would support the tyranny that we fought against in the Second World War. I could understand why some sieg heiled and I think most Skinheads of that time would have done it for a laugh to upset the establishment, but there were those that believed it.

I had friends who were right wing, I had friends who were left wing, friends who were anarchists. I believed the idea of Oi was working class and that was left wing, But the far right had been attending punk gigs way before Oi arrived, Sham 69 had a lot of right wing skinheads following them, they didn't want them, but that's how it was.

Football was the same, Chelsea and the Head-hunters and Combat 18. It was when the right wing started to turn up at Reggae do's and cause trouble that clashes would happen. It went off at Cock Sparrer at the Astoria in 1992, the band had played a blinding set with strippers, the Addicts came on as we were leaving and Monkey was Naked, taking the piss, all hell broke loose as a lot of blood and honour were there as the next day it all kicked off at Waterloo station.

I remember being at a Desmond Dekker gig with my wife, and a group of lads in front of us, one bone head started sieg heiling and giving Desmond abuse. I just steamed in, we had paid 15 quid for the tickets and I presume so had he, I could never work out why he didn't stand outside and protest.

Favourite bands include The Specials, as they influenced me into the music and the skinhead way of life, then Last Resort, Cock Sparrer, 4 skins and the Rejects. On the punk side I suppose the Clash and the Ruts. Today I DJ and mostly listen to Original Reggae (skinhead reggae), Ska and Rocksteady. Now from that period it has to be the Maytals, Slim Smith, Hot Rod All-stars, but it's more about the tunes than the bands. The pioneers did some great tunes, but also some pony ones.

BARRY TRACEY

In the spring of 1969 my world changed for the better. The top 30 charts normally treated with disdain by the youth of our age suddenly started to be something worth looking forward to on a Sunday evening. In the local cafes', youth clubs, and on the transistor radios on the bus on the way to school (owned by the better-off kids than myself) in the morning Desmond Dekker was King! The Israelites ruled our air waves, ably supported as spring turned into summer by the likes of the Upsetters, Jimmy Cliff, Johnny Nash, Harry J and the All-stars, the Pioneers and one certain Max Romeo! All charted in or around the top 40, with Double D having a number one and number two that year. However, Max Romeos 'Wet Dream' was the song we all wanted to hear. Unfortunately 'Auntie Beeb' had decided the lyrics to this tune were just too much for a nation of stick in the mud types, so it was cafés and youth clubs only (unless you bought the single) for the likes of me and you. I was only 12 that year but I was fortunate enough to have another three brothers, of which two of them were older than me.

In 1969, much to my poor mother's chagrin, her record player was taken over and Elvis, Petula Clark and Jack Jones were removed from the deck, to be replaced day and night by the 'Children's choice' that was Ska music. I 'acquired' Brixton Cat Big and Fat by Dice the Boss and I was hooked for life. 1969 came and went far too quickly for myself and my mates, who were bored to death of having to listen to the likes of Ken Dodd and Rolf Harris topping the charts.

That summer, however, my 16 year old brother had come home one day with a skinhead haircut, Doctor Marten boots and Ben Sherman shirt. He looked the dog's gonads and I was right up for heading out to get the same cut and clothes, having two paper rounds at the time which would have financed it. There the dream ended, when my mother put her foot down and forbade it, as I was the only child in our family of six kids who had made it to grammar school. The clothes she accepted when out of school uniform, but the 'cut' didn't happen until my later years.

Before you knew it, 69 had been and gone, and it only seemed a blink of an eye before Slade, T Rex and The Sweet were kings of the top 30. Was I a skinhead back then? The simple answer is no. In spirit maybe I was, but for a cruel twist of fate that saw me pass my 11+. There have been wilderness years between then and now, dictated such by the likes of bringing up two separate families, having married twice over that period of time. In recent years my love for the music and the scene has been probably beyond reason at times (my ex-wives' comments) but it's good to be fully back. Skinheads never die they just grow old, someone once said. I say amen to that. Keep the Faith.

PAUL BOND

 I became a skinhead after seeing Madness on TOTP performing 'The Prince' in 1979! I was immediately hooked with both the ska sound and the clothes they were wearing.

I had listened to quite a lot of reggae and was into the new wave/punk sound. Madness and The Specials seemed to embrace the two, perfect dance music! I straight away upset mother by getting a grade 4 crop and got my first Harrington jacket which was gradually covered in Madness and Two Tone patches bought from our local market.

I moved from Surrey back down to Brixham in Devon in 1983 and met up with the Brixham skins, a bunch of lads ranging from 14 to 20 years. There were about 10 in our crew, this is when I realised what being a skin was all about.

I then got more into older 60's ska like Toots and the Maytals, Prince Busted, Desmond Dekker and Trojan! Such good music! The Oi! scene also played a big part in these years (no- nonsense, in-your-face street punk!!) Brixham, especially in winter, is a very quiet town where everyone knows everyone so we rarely witnessed any trouble or violence towards us but the summer months were quite different! The population of the town probably tripled with 'grockles' from every part of the UK. We had a few run-ins with groups of lads but nothing major. Mostly it was good natured piss taking of the invaders to our little town.

Racism was something we never had dealings with, we had two half cast lads in our crew (who were from the only coloured family in the town!) dressed exactly like us! I guess being away from the big cities, we didn't have any experience of living in a mixed race society.

The best part of being a skinhead was the tight knit group you belonged to, nothing was too much trouble. If you were skint, your mate would buy you a pint, if you were in trouble everyone was behind you, you were never alone.

I also loved the scornful looks on the older generation's faces when 10 or more skins stomped up through the street in 14 hole Docs, rolled up jeans and number one crops. A sight to behold.

Brixham is a fishing town: most of our boys had connection to the industry. 1985 saw the sinking of a crab boat in the channel when we lost two of our crew, their bodies were never found! This was the lowest time for the Brixham skinheads.

I'm going to be 50 this year but still dress the same, listen to ska and punk daily and play drums in a ska/punk/new wave covers band called Oldage Kicks. I will always be a skinhead (nature has helped with the hair situation!) and hope my kids grow up with the same feelings of loyalty from their mates!

CHRIS RICHARDSON

 I became a skinhead in 1979. I was into northern soul, my mate's brother who was 10 years older than us was a skinhead in 69. After meeting him and seeing the clothes he wore (boots and braces) he took us to see a reggae band. When we got in to the club it was packed with skinheads. That was it for me, went home, shaved my head, got the ox bloods on, braces on.

Started seeing reggae bands and still going to northern soul all-nighters, which skinheads used to go to as well, so the skinheads followed reggae and northern soul. As for ska, that was left to the rude boys and suedehead and some skinheads. Being a skinhead to me was to belong to the best subculture in the world-- you only have to go into a pub to see another skinhead u don't know and it's a nod of the head to each other's family.

Most memorable moment -and there are many- but if I had to pick one it would be Weston bank holiday: 500 skinheads on a bank holiday listening to reggae, drinking beer, and dancing on the beach front.

As for violence, I encountered a lot, but the one that always sticks in my mind was when we had gone to a club to see a reggae band, got the dates mixed up and ended up in a club full of rockers. We were in there for 10 mins before the first bottle was thrown at us, then we let loose with the ox bloods and bar stools. The fight spilled out on the street on Swindon which then turned in to a pitch battle and had to fight our way out to the train station, resulting in me having a broken nose, eye socket, and wrist -win some, lose some - -as it goes, lol.

We came in to conflict with bone heads at a pub in Swindon called the Moonraker, they started chanting racist shit, we took pool cues to them, another punch up in a car park with them .As for music, Toots and the Maytals, the Pioneers, Symarip Jim Kelly, Ethiopians and northern soul. As for the clothes: brogues, bencher man short sleeve shirts Fred Perry, Harringtons, and Levi jeans

BILL NEWBERRY

I was bought up on reggae n ska, my mum n dad were both 69 skins and me dad loved a scooter so it's my blood. I became a skinhead when I was 16 and got a lammy for my 17th, so that's where it all began for me. I loved being a young skinhead in my era coz u stood out from the crowd n felt important which wasn't really that long ago, coz

I'm only 30 now. Just lacing ya boots up b4 goin for a stomp around Chatham high street used to make me feel 10 feet tall. WORKING CLASS AND PROUD.

On the music side, I'm a big reggae nerd and not just skinhead reggae either, I love it all: Lee Scratch Perry every time for me. I don't think you can beat reggae music. I've had the odd scuffle ere n there wiv prats --mainly in kebab shops n shit like that when I'm on way home from a reggae do. Saying that, I had scuffle at the last ska shack do, due to spilling a pint on a local in the pub. Sorry mate, skinhead is a way of life for me. I live n breath it every day and it will always be a big part of my life spirit of 69.

JIM LEWIS

Skinhead started for me in early 1980, I loved the look and the music (2 Tone). The first single I bought was a 12 inch of 'Too Much Too Young'. It was no different from the 7inch version, but it was a Jap import with a Jap lyric sheet. I was 10 years old and still own it.

Being a skinhead to me is the love of the music, the love of the look, it's part of your soul, it's something that becomes engrained in you. Once you have it, it never leaves: it's a way of life.

The most memorable experience as a skinhead was going to the Specials 30th reunion tour at Margate 2009, I had only been doing the skinhead thing again for about 4 years. Me and my mate Si went down for the gig, we thought we were 2 of only a handful of skins that were left..... How very wrong we were... The Westcoast was full of fucking skinheads... I couldn't believe what I was seeing

I never encountered much in the way of violence as a skin in the 80s, we were only lads... I do remember a time when we got into a bit of a scrap with some mods, when a friend of mine wrapped a bike chain around his hand and punched one in the face... It was nasty... And something I am not proud to have witnessed... Cuntish. I have never come into conflict with racist skinheads... I don't know any, and I don't want to.

DEBBIE JONES

When I was 14 in 1978 I became a skinhead and it was because I was already into the music and lots of kids in my year were getting into it. One of the boys formed the Loafers who backed Laurel Aitken a lot. I was already into ska because we had a Jamaican family at the end of our street. I used to hang out there with a boy from my year and his parents always had music playing-- all original ska-- so I was already into it before the 2 Tone movement started.

Being a skinhead to me is a way of life, it's about music, style and we are one big family with a common love of the culture. It's been hard over the years and still is now to some extent because people just don't get it, they still think we are all racist thugs which couldn't be further from the truth.

My most memorable moments are meeting my idols over the years, met and seeing pretty much everyone I love perform at least once at some point. Also the times I have spent with the skinhead family at some great music weekends. Bad moments include being at a Specials gig about 1981, I think, when a load of national front guys started a riot and the gig had to be abandoned to protect the band, Neville in particular. Also other scary times early on when the national front was big and if you didn't join them, you were targeted. Also in the last few years in Camden a load of Eastern Europeans had us trapped in the Elephants Head pub where we used to go very Sunday. They started to incite violence early evening by handing out national front material and giving us the Nazi salute.

FRANK STRUVE

I became a skinhead in spring 1982. I became a skinhead because I could identify with the basic premises, being working class and proud. What happened was I became a punk first, and then a heavy metal dude, none of which quite suited me. Then a guy called Jesper asked me if I wanted to go to Århus town party. Jesper was a skinhead, so I knew the basics of the style. And of course I knew 2-tone and a bit of Oi! While in Århus, people explained to me what skinheads were all about, got introduced to old-school ska. I heard Desmond Dekker and The Symarips.

At the time I had shoulder-length hair, and the second or third day, someone got a couple of sheep shears and took my hair off. Tore it off, it felt more like. That's how I got my first number one crop. I had a t-shirt and a pair of jeans that I rolled up. I hadn't any boots, so someone gave me their old, beaten DM's that were held together with gaffer-tape. I sure was a sight for sore eyes! Needless to say, they didn't polish up so well! I had to wait for a year before anyone from Denmark went to England, and brought a pair of proper DM 14 holes home for me. There wasn't any internet at the time, as you might recall, so we waited until someone from Denmark went to London and then we all ordered new gear from them. If you went to England, you almost had to carry an empty suitcase, just to bring back orders from the rest of the crew.

The three experiences that stand out the most, was definitely my first trip to London. I went with a couple of mates: we stayed in Regent's Palace in Piccadilly Circus.

The almost magical experience of standing by the end of Carnaby Street and looking, and there was stores that sold donkey jackets and Crombie's and Sta-Prest and you just squawked like a school boy in a whorehouse. I ended up buying my first Ben Sherman and my first Sta-Prest. I had the trousers sewn up in the shop. I also bought a pair of DM loafers. We ended up outside Merc's, drooling, went inside (still drooling), and saw for the first time a tonic suit (drool!), which we obviously couldn't afford. After the shopping spree we had to digest everything, so we went into a kiosk and bought 12 Special Brew, and ended up by the fountain in Piccadilly Circus, singing 'Special Brew' by Bad Manners.

The second memorable thing was when we went to Lübeck, Germany to see Indecent Exposure. There was also a German band called Böhse Onkelz playing, we just went on this trip for the music. We arrived the day before the gig, where we met a German skinhead who introduced himself as Ratze. We stayed with him that weekend. Saturday, the day of the gig, there was arranged buses to where the concerts would play. We went with the Lübeck Skins to the train station to pick up the skins from Berlin. When the train arrived and the doors opened, out came two or three hundred skinheads, everybody was chanting "Skin-head! Skin-head! Skin-head!"! The hairs of the back of my neck stood up.

After that, it rather went downhill, it turned out that half of them were Boneheads, unfortunately. We were in the middle of nowhere when we realized, so we just kept our heads down and went back to Ratze's place afterwards. He wasn't a Nazi. Sunday afternoon we just went to the Lübeck train station and pissed off back to Denmark, and I haven't been in Lübeck since.

The third, and last, was in 2011, when I got married to my wife in Margate, with our English skinhead family as witnesses. The Rev David Ireland was our minister. It was a beautiful day, and we hadn't even arranged as much as a bouquet, much less a cake. Everything fucked up, my wife forgot to give me the ring, my wife waited for ages outside the door, she was waiting for the music to start, we were waiting for her to come in, and people started joking that they had seen her take the train out of Margate. I tell you, I wasn't half sweating! Earlier, I popped a button off my suit jacket as I bent down to polish my brogues. Needless to say, it didn't feel much like my lucky day, at that point. But every day afterwards have been pure marital bliss, so who cares.

I have had conflicts with racists, but it hasn't been skinheads, it's been colleagues, friends, and family. It's not that I am afraid of conflict, or that I don't possess the right arguments, it is rather that participating in an argument with a racist always makes me feel slightly more stupid, as if stupidity is contagious through conflict.

It's hard to pick favourites with clothing, because I love the skinhead gear. As much as I like slacking off in a pair of jeans, I also love putting on a tonic suit. I like my Harrington's, but I also love my Crombie's. Can't pick anything out, mate. I like the 80's Oi!, but I love the ska music, old and younger.

I have been in fights, not because I am a skinhead, but because I believed it to be necessary. For example, when a mate and me saw two greasers attack an elderly gentleman who just got out of a cab. I cannot let a thing like that pass. Or like the time three young men were in a pub and verbally abused the waitress. I pulled one of them by his tie, across the table, out of the pub. It turned out that the three of them were police academy students, which didn't get them any advance. The only time I have been in a fight as a skinhead, because I was a skinhead, against other skins, was when a group of Swedish skinheads went to Copenhagen because they thought they would show the Danish "Disco- skins" -as they called us, seeing as we did dress proper, not just in Oi! Gear- who the true Vikings were. That didn't go over too well, as we told them in no uncertain terms, that that is the Danes. There have been other fights: we skinheads seem to attract them, but no time to tell all the tall tales. I've won a fair amount, but also lost more than I care to think about.

WAYNE SMITH

For me it all started in 1979, off the back of being a punk. It just felt right to me as if that was what I was meant to be, if you like, and that's what I've remained to this day. Great mates, great music, great contacts, FAMILY is the way it feels to me.

Musically I like a massive range of stuff, but my main love is for all things SKA, be it rock steady, lovers rock, or even 2 Tone.

My first experience of skinheads was going up to secondary school at 11 years old and seeing the older 16 year old lads and thinking 'fuck me they look the dogs bollox'. That was it-- my future was mapped out for me. I was to be a life-long skinhead.

There have been many, many, violent actions all over the country but I'll always remember the first big occasion. I had been told that loads of skinhead got together at Skegness sea side resort in Lincolnshire, so at 14 years old I was the only skinhead in my town now, so had a word with my mate who was a punk and that was it- off we went on the train to Derby to catch the Skegness train. We boarded the train and sat down with all the families off to the coast for the day. However, we weren't sat there long before a massive skinhead, much older than we were, came past and said 'follow me, skin, we have got our own carriage down here' and, sure enough, about 50 skins had their own carriage. Beer was given to us and we were away- let the journey begin.

As we arrived in Skegness we came out of the station and across the road to the Lumley Hotel pub, there was already about 300 skins in there and it was lively when a skin came in and shouted that a skinhead had been stabbed on the seafront. There was an explosion of skins trashing the pub and trying to get out all at the same time, we were an army surging down the road heading for the sea front, crushing everyone and everything that got in our way. The adrenalin was running, I was up for anything now- there was no stopping me.

We had a good few hours fighting with the Mods and then the coppers on the sea front before all being rounded up and put on one train all together to get us out of the town. I remember seeing the guard on the train locking himself inside the cargo cage out of the way. Anything we could smash out of the train got thrown out of the windows at cars on level crossings. The cord was constantly being pulled and the train stopped so skins could run from the train .Well that was the start of regular bank holiday visits to various sea side resorts all over the country. Great times indeed.

Things are a lot more civilized these days. I love the SKA nights that I attend around the country, it's now all about respect, clothing, music and mates that you can trust with your life but don't be fooled. When you look round that room at the ageing skinhead there in front of you there is a volcano of passion and aggression just waiting to explode when the day comes. Hard times- hard men- hard skinheads never die.

ROSS FERGUS CROFT

It was 1992 when I became a skinhead. I was 15 living in Handsworth in Birmingham with my mate Wolfy's family. Our next door neighbour, Noris, was an old Jamaican rude boy straight from the 60's. He was the coolest bloke I'd ever seen in his blue tonic suit and pork pie hat. We used to help him with odd jobs as both of us had been kicked out of school. He used to play us his old ska and soul records and, if I'm honest, let us dip into his weed pot. He told us old stories about him and his skinhead mates, showed us old pictures with the weed and Toots and the Maytals tunes. We were both hooked

Photo © Ross Fergus Croft with daughter Betty Rose Croft

Now as all real skinheads will attest to: being smart, hard-working, proud, working class and standing up for yourself and your loved ones is what being a real skinhead is all about.

Some of my most memorable experiences – good and bad – include

the first time I wore tonic suit and brogues out on the piss. I did well with the ladies, though.

Getting the shit kicked out of me by 20 Asians in Nottingham because I had docs on, didn't seem to matter to them that I had a badge with a picture of Derrick Morgan. By the way, I hold no grudge, my best mate's Asian and an ex royal marine, so he can kick the shit out of them, haha.

Yes, I admit I was quite violent when I was younger. One point, me, my brothers and mates (not all skins) would hang out in pubs we knew boneheads would drink in and give them a taste of their own medicine. Nowadays I'm a happy family man and would rather educate, but sometimes you got to do what you got to do.

Yes, I have conflict with racist skinheads. The first time is when I moved back to Norfolk from Birmingham. I've still got the scars on my knuckles!

DAVE BOSS GRIFFITH

Photo © Dave Griffin with Suggs from Madness

Back in my early youth I remember my mother having some reggae records, one being *Monkey Spanner*, which I played to death. In 1978, being 14, I was waiting to go to school and Prince Buster's 'Al Capone' came on the radio and blew me away. Then in 1979, the Two Tone explosion happened and I was hooked. That year I went to see Madness at Deeside leisure centre, which introduced me to the Skinhead look.

1983 I got my first Scooter and off on the Mod Rallies we went. I was not into the scruffy look of the National rallies. Good old Tony Class did not play many Ska or Boss tunes, but it was always worth the trips. The only trouble I really encountered was the Lincoln rally "Mod story by Me". I still own four of my Scooters, one being the love of my life 1967 Lambretta SX200 Special.

My music is Ska, Boss Reggae, Northern Soul and a bit of Punk. I love everything about being a Skinhead, it's like a big Ska family. My main clothes are Docs, (God knows how many pairs), Fred Perry's, Ben Sherman's, braces and Pork Pie hats. Last year I started Deejaying "Boss Sounds", playing all my music and getting paid for doing it

STEVE CAMPBELL

I was into my punk and still like the old school punk. However, I became interested in the skin scene way back in the eighties, the cleanliness, the sharp dress, and pride of how you look, the music and comradeship. But most of all getting together and having a proper laugh with no grief. The non-fascist racist bullshit, I don't do political shit, colour, religion, creed-- just friendship, laughs, and music, that's what being a skinhead means to me.

I remember getting the shit kicked out of me twice in one month by a group of blokes that thought I was someone else, cunts. But yes, great gigs, especially in my home town of Margate. Too many good times to mention. Oh, and I can recall having a punch up at the Specials gig in Margate when someone started on my boy.

Yes I've had quite a few scraps, but always defended my mates, myself, and my beliefs. I am no racist, homophobic, political, or anything- just me.

I've had conflicts with racist skinheads but also just general society. I fucking hate racists. My ex-wife was mixed race, therefore my children are and I won't tolerate any of that shit.

Love all ska, reggae, blue beat. I still love my punk and Oi! -- loving the feckin ejits. The Warriors. And most working man's Oi!, non-racist of course.

Love my shorts, crisp ironed and creased jeans, Tonic suits, hand-made brogue boots 'n shoes, polished docs and Crombie, not to mention my original 1970's American MA1 Flight jacket.

REV DAVE IRELAND

My Story – Rev David Ireland (AKA. The Rev)

When and why did I become a Skinhead?

My mum was a Mod in the 60s and for most of my childhood, I was surrounded by the music of that genre. I was raised on bands like The Small Faces and the Kinks, but also by genres such as Motown, R&B, Northern Soul and, of course, Reggae and Ska. One of the first records I recall hearing (and learning) was Johnny Reggae by the Piglets.

As a result of this, up until the age of about 11, I had no interest in the music that was in the charts or played on the radio in the 70s. Then I saw THAT episode of Top of The Pops and seeing The Specials and Madness was a revelation, here were bands of my generation playing the sort of music I was brought up on, I convinced mum to buy me a Harrington from the local market and that was it......I was hooked, I've never looked back. Although my mum still refers to me as a 'Hard or Peanut Mod'.

When and How Did I Become a Reverend – And Peoples' Reaction?

I've always been a person of faith, an Irish Catholic, but initially this had nothing to do with the Reverend Title.

On and off, I've DJ'd at Skinhead/Scooterist events for the best part of 25 years. In 2009 I was asked if I would DJ for the Sunday afternoon of the Big 40 event in Margate (this turned out to be a 12 hour session). When I DJ, I like to talk to the crowd, get them going, mention friends in the room, get them up etc. For me, there is nothing more boring than DJs who just play song after song and say nothing. As a result, my sets at Big 40 events became known as The Sunday Sermon and I was christened The Rev by the crowd.

In 2010, I was approached by two friends from Denmark who wished to get married, but wanted the wedding to be as Skinhead as possible, after a few conversations between us and a 12 month online ordination course, I was a fully blown reverend and conducted their wedding in 2011. I think I was more nervous than they were.

Peoples' reaction to me being a Skinhead and a reverend usually gravitate towards sheer disbelief, but most of the UK Skinheads know who and what I am, and I like to think that they are secretly quite proud to have their very own clergyman in their ranks. I've never received a negative reaction from the Skinhead community and they have never given me any disrespect regarding my openness of faith.

Only one non-skinhead has ever been disrespectful to me regarding my faith, but he soon found out that although I am a reverend, I am still a Skinhead and that in this case, a punch was more effective than a prayer. I think I actually quoted the following verse to him:

"The LORD is a jealous and avenging God, The LORD avengeth and is full of wrath; The LORD taketh vengeance

on His adversaries, And He reserveth wrath for His enemies."

What does being a skinhead mean to you?

Being a Skinhead means everything to me. I wake up, I'm a Skinhead. I go to work, I'm a Skinhead. I wear Skinhead clothes at all times, there's never a time when I'm not a Skinhead. I revel in being the smartest geezer in the pub. As Judge Dread sung – "Say what you like, he's the king of the streets".

Many things have come and gone in my life; houses, girlfriends, cars and wives, but being a Skinhead has always been a constant and my Skinhead family (cos that's what we are) has ALWAYS been there for me and I know they ALWAYS will be.

What are some of your most memorable experiences as a skinhead (good and bad)?

I have so many memorable experiences; I couldn't begin to list them here. As a DJ, getting to DJ for and know the bands I worshipped as a youngster, such as The Beat, Bad Manners, The Selecter has been both memorable and an honour. I also got to dance on stage with the late, great Desmond Dekker shortly before he was taken from us.

The only negative is constantly being perceived as a racist. It gets quite tiresome having to educate the ignorant.

Do you find being a reverend often crosses over into the skinhead world - such as performing wedding ceremonies for skinheads?

My status as a reverend stems totally from my faith and from the Skinhead community. Nearly all my reverential duties are in the Skinhead world. I'm non-incumbent at the moment

(I don't have a parish) so I like to think of the worldwide Skinhead community as my congregation.

I've performed several weddings and blessings for Skinhead couples, but thankfully no funerals yet. I never charge for my services, but if people want to pay my expenses, that's great. If they can't afford to – that's fine too. It's not about money, as that would be wrong – it's about faith and love.

People should also be aware that just because they are Skinheads, it doesn't mean that I will automatically perform a ceremony for them. I have to get to know them: I have to know they are serious. If they tell me they are atheists, I won't do it. It is not a gimmick, it's not a laugh – it's my faith and I take it extremely seriously, nearly as seriously as I take being a Skinhead.

DAVID WEBSTER

Photo © David Webster with his sons Troy
And Garth with reggae legends Monty and
Roy Ellis

I guess I was destined to become a skinhead from an early age. My upbringing was a tough one where I was surrounded by violence. My Dad was a veteran of WW2, a Docker, and a boozer, one not to pick an argument with.

I must have been about 10/11 years of age when I saw older boys and girls wearing clothing against the norm, clothing and indeed appearances, I would describe as "being of a tough nature". Very short, cropped hair styles, checked shirts, braces, jeans taken up- exposing either Dr Marten or Monkey boots. I remember my reaction being one of, "Wow,

198

they look hard," and wishing I was older so that I could look like that. I remember pestering my Mum for a crew cut hair style and a pair of boots. No such luck!

It was around this period I discovered the Richard Allen novels depicting the life of fictional skinhead Joe Hawkins, I read the lot. It wasn't long before the skinheads grew their hair as the Glam rock scene took over. The 1970s, it seemed, had everything, from Glam to Tamla Motown, from Reggae to Rock, it was all there. By 1972ish Skinheads were passé, yesterday's news.

It was during the early/mid 70s that I began attending local discos. My hair was long, which was the fashion then, but the footwear was always DMs. It was during this period that I discovered the sounds of Desmond Dekker, Dave and Ansel Collins and Dandy Livingstone, sounds that knocked me off my feet. Alas, I was to become a punk!!!

In 1976 Punk Rock hit the headlines, a new cult was born. By now I was 18 years of age, full of attitude, and a very angry young man. I immediately got into the punk scene. I attended my first- ever, what I would call 'proper', gig: The Clash at Bath Pavilion. That was it, I was hooked, music and gigs were to take over my life. I was to be heavily influenced by the arrival of 2 Tone.

The defining moment was a Cockney Rejects gig in Exeter in early 1980. This was the moment I was to see Skinheads en masse for the first time. They literally took over the venue: fights were breaking out in every corner, with skinheads being the perpetrators and indeed victors. The next day I was to have a number one crop, closely followed by around 10 others from the town where i lived [Watchet in Somerset]. Within months there were about 30 of us from the Minehead/Taunton area.

Which brings me to the question "What does being a skinhead mean to me? Being a skinhead was certainly not a passing fashion for me, as the course of time has proven! 35 years on and I am still heavily into the scene. 35 years of many ups and many downs. Being part of it has been my life: I have met some of the most loyal, genuine, fun-filled people it is possible to imagine. I have also met some of the most evil, vicious and most unsavoury scumbags on the planet. Thankfully the latter are in the minority.

It gives me great pleasure in describing being a skinhead as being a part of a family. I really cannot put it any clearer than that. That is the ultimate accolade I can pay to this culture, which has been my way of life for so long. I felt for the first time in my life I was amongst friends, proper friends that would literally put their lives on the line for me, as I would them. We all shared a common interest: which was our love of music, our taste in clothing, and our undying loyalty for each other. We would drink, dance and fight together as one, giving us a feeling of invincibility.

My pals and I would enjoy many nights out at gigs throughout the late 70s/early 80s, seeing bands such as The Angelic Upstarts, The Jam, Dexy's Midnight Runners, The Specials, Madness and Bad Manners. Trouble was usually not too far away. This was Thatcher's Britain, a violent Britain, a Britain dominated by divide. We had wars in Ireland and the Falklands, Poll tax riots, miners' strikes, and racism on a grand scale.

Coming from a small town in Somerset, my pals and I had never encountered racism. Why would we when there were no residents of foreign blood living in the area, at least none we knew of, or indeed cared about. It was attending 2 Tone gigs of that period that hit it home that there were massive problems in Britain regarding racial issues. As much as the Specials and their like tried to bring all people together regardless of colour, the more it seemed trouble would kick off. Helped massively by the right wing tabloids that portrayed ALL skinheads as everything bad. In the eyes of the media, skinheads were glue sniffing, sieg heiling, granny bashing thugs. Which was far from the truth.

My most memorable experiences as a skinhead, good and bad. Now this question warrants a book alone. My 35/40 years of being into the scene have been more or less my life, so the question really is my most memorable experiences of my life. Would have to begin with the Cockney Rejects gig of the late 70s as being my first memorable experience. From then on it's been one hell of a roller coaster ride.

On the good side, a ride of meeting some bloody good mates, seeing some of the best bands planet Earth has ever witnessed, being married to the most gorgeous skinhead girl ever, who gave me 4 terrific sons, watching my sons grow up, being there for them, the list of good things in my life could go on and on. If I had to pick out the most memorable gigs I have attended, most of them would be a blank, due to my intake of alcohol, a vice that was to be my downfall in so many respects. I saw just about every skinhead band, Oi! and ska, punk and 2 Tone, rock and reggae, that I had wished to, giving me absolute pleasure many would take for granted.

On the other side of the coin, the bad experiences of my life have also left a mark which at times is hard to shake off. I have served many custodial sentences, which account for approximately over 4 years of my life, almost all brought on by my addiction to alcohol, as was the break-up of my marriage. I left Somerset in late 1981, after serving a 3 month prison sentence in HMP Exeter for the crime of causing actual bodily harm. On my release I turned my back on my county of birth Somerset, to move to the city where it was all happening, London, my brother and girlfriend of that period having secured a bedsit for me in Slough, just on the outskirts of the capital. It was like the beginning of a new life, with new mates, new job, new surroundings and what was to be a new realisation of a life completely different from anything I had known in the West Country. Being a skinhead, I was soon to be welcomed into the pack of fellow skinheads in Hounslow, West London, and my tenure in Slough being very temporary. I was averaging 3/4 gigs a week, mainly Oi type bands, the Business, 4 Skins, Last Resort, but also bands with a more sinister motive.

I was asked if I would like to attend a Skrewdriver gig at London's 100 club in October of 1982. A band that at that time I had never heard of. I was gobsmacked at what I was to witness. There were masses of right arms in the air doing Nazi salutes. My initial reaction was one of shock. After all, my father had served Britain in World War 2, fighting against the probability of a Nazi invasion. As the beer flowed and with the camaraderie in abundance, thoughts of rationality vanished. I found myself mesmerised by the words of the bands' lead singer. I was still relatively new to London and once again felt I was being welcomed into a new family. This was indeed a strange period of my life in many respects: almost like I was being false to myself, as deep down I knew I did not hate people for the colour of their skin.

For in between being present at Skrewdriver/Combat 84/Brutal Attack gigs, I would also be at such gigs as Desmond Dekker/Prince Buster and Laurel Aitken, as well as at gigs of a more leftish allegiance, such as Conflict/Subhumans and the Angelic Upstarts. One such concert I was at was very memorable, and, I suspect, one to stay in the minds of all present. I went along to the GLC Festival in London's Jubilee Gardens in June of 1984, where one of the bands playing, The Redskins, were to take one hell of a beating. It was a free event, so I went along with my girlfriend of the time, Jacky. What I witnessed can only be described as an organised stage invasion, planned to precision. About 20 minutes into the Redskins set, all hell went loose. From where I was standing it almost looked like a swarm of locusts flying through the air towards the band. It was, in fact, hundreds of bottles. The entire field erupted as many skinheads attacked the band and their crew. Fights were going off everywhere. It was a battlefield. I just grabbed Jacky and got as far away as I could. I have been in many situations where violence has taken place, but nothing on this scale.

Which brings me to the next question concerning racial and political views: Whether one agrees or disagrees, likes it or not, there is no denying that politics and skinheads go hand in hand. It was simply not possible to avoid politics when the lyrics of so many 2 Tone and Oi songs were based on the reality of what was occurring throughout the nation. The subject of racism was never very far away.

As I have said earlier, the influence of seeing Skrewdriver perform at London's 100 club had an instant impact on my way of thinking, as it did on just about every other skinhead I knew at that time. I was simply so damned ignorant and stubborn then to realise that any form of hatred was negative. The situation was not helped by a certain tabloid, which just happens to be Britain's biggest seller, hyping the issue into something monstrous. It was almost as if this tabloid got a buzz out of stirring up stories of a racial theme. This tabloid would portray ALL skinheads as Thatcher's storm troopers. It was so easy to be taken in, and yes even manipulated by such stories.

The right wing parties were to play a huge part in many skinheads' lives, playing on the fact that many were gullible and easily led to believe that having racial tendencies was the way forward. Which obviously is not the case!!! I was present at many gigs where violence occurred because of race. And it was not always white on black. In October of 1983, myself, a friend and our girl friends were threatened and then chased around Hammersmith by a gang of black youths, where we took refuge in a pub, after we were on our way to a UB40/Winston Reedy gig at Hammersmith's Odeon. The threat of being attacked by black or Asian gangs simply for being a skinhead was a reality throughout the 1980s, such was the influence from the biased media. For black skinheads, the threat was double, where they faced the wrath of right wing skinheads, along with the anger of other black youth. I believe it was mainly race issues that almost killed off the skinhead scene in the mid-1990s, many skinheads becoming fed up of being branded as racists, many other skinheads coming to their senses and finally grasping the fact that their views were hypocritical and pointless to say the least.

It was during the 90s that I appeared on a TV debate show, *Kilroy,* where the subject of the show was racism. I had made my mind up that I was going to denounce racism for what I believed it was. As I entered the Teddington Studios Green rooms, I could not fail to notice that the audience were over 80% black, with many black celebrities present, including politicians, sports promoter Ambrose Mendy, boxer Nigel Benn, and former footballer John Fashanu.

The looks I got as I entered the Green room were enough to kill: it was as if I had been immediately stereotyped as being a racist. 10 minutes in to the show, and remember it was a live show; I got my chance to speak. I explained that many skinheads that swear allegiance to right wing parties were hypocrites and false because of the way they claimed to enjoy music that originated from the West Indies, for the way they begin their day by purchasing a newspaper from an Asian newsagent and ending their day by tucking into a Turkish kebab.

I went on to state that I had witnessed racial attacks of 6 on to one, which had turned my stomach and that I felt helpless to help the victim. Attacks that left me feeling deeply ashamed afterwards. I had been warned before I went on the show that I would suffer much grief afterwards, but the reality was I felt a huge weight had been lifted from me. John Fashanu approached me afterwards, shook my hand uttering, "Respect to you man, that must have taken some bottle".

I remember the following weekend, as I was cold shouldered by two supposed skinhead friends as I entered the Elephants Head in Camden. But for every one that gave me abuse, ten more would applaud me for saying what I did. I feel there really is no room for racism in a progressing society. Yet there are still those that refuse to budge from their views, those stuck in a time warp, beating themselves up over issues they cannot win. Yes, these people still exist!! I would describe myself today as a patriot, l love to see my country win, whether it's Mo Farah in the 10,000 metres or Lewis Hamilton at Formula One. We are a multicultural nation and nothing is ever going to change that. As I stated earlier, the skinhead scene almost died in the 90s, for a variety of reasons, the main reason in my opinion was issues concerning race. Yet the scene re- emerged at the beginning of the 2000s with ska, reggae and 2Tone at the front.

The scene today is so much better in many respects. The fear of being attacked or arrested is almost non-existent today, skinheads are no longer put into the category of racists. There are ska tribute bands, and yes, even original bands performing almost every weekend around the country. The scene is buzzing and people are smiling. Over the last 5 years many older skinheads are getting back into it, there are younger generation skinheads without a thought of racism in their heads, the hatred has gone.

Being a skinhead from the late 70s, right through the 80s and 90s, right up to the present day, I cannot help but notice the vast changes in the manner in which our streets, our way of life, our attitudes, our characters have changed.

Violence and being a skinhead went together, like salt and pepper. It followed us like a shadow, it was unavoidable. Going back to the early days of skinheads, there were many causes that instigated violence, it may have been because of race, or a turf war over territory. Hounslow skinheads were very territorial, having had many battles with skinheads from other boroughs. It may have been violence towards other cults. I personally remember the run-ins we used to have with biker gangs in Somerset, before I moved to London, which sometimes got very nasty with weapons used.

Bank Holidays at Weston-Super-Mare were always periods of much violence, with the animosity between Bristol and Bath skinheads at the forefront. In many situations violence would erupt over political views. Skinhead/Punk gigs in London in the 1980s almost always had the odd scrap or two. Sometimes over girlfriends, skinheads were, and still are very protective over their women.

There were a variety of reasons that triggered violence. But it was a tag much associated with the skinhead cult. There is no denying the fact that skinheads, including myself in my younger days, enjoyed fighting. Even when beat we would have a laugh about it afterwards. I lost count of the amount of fights I was involved in, the stitches I had, the black eyes and the bruises I suffered. There was certainly no rule book when it came to violence: Queensberry rules were non-existent. Very rarely was there a one against one situation.

Police brutality was also very rife during the 1980s. I was at a Business gig in Coventry at the Hand on Heart public house, where around 50 plus police officers lost the plot in going mental with their batons. I myself was left in a heap on the floor. The Business then went on to record a song about the event. I was at a Specials gig at Bristol Locarno in 1979, where the venue seemed to break into one mass brawl. It really was literally happening at every gig.

Much of the violence was fuelled by alcohol, there always seemed to be booze at the root of it. I know that was the case with myself. But the fact remains that, like so many things in life, getting pissed was all part of skinhead life. Alcohol changes people, it makes them do and say things they would never dream of doing or saying. Put the three ingredients together, Skinhead-Alcohol-Politics, and it's a recipe for trouble. It took me many years to realise this problem. I drank my last drop of alcohol on April 12th 2006, the best thing I have ever done in my life. The proof is in the pudding, or so they say and I can honestly say quitting the booze has changed me completely, not once in 10 years of sobriety have I raised a fist in anger, any hatreds or grudges I may have harboured in the past now gone.

My big regret, and it really is a massive regret, is that I did not quit alcohol 30 years ago! I can go to a gig now and remember everything about it, every song played, every person I spoke to. Compare that to my early days of being a skinhead when much of life is a void, a blank in my mind. No more worrying about who I had upset or punched the night before.

Life is good, the skinhead scene is good, yep many of us still involved in it are now 30/40 years older, but we are involved in friendships that have stood the test of time. Many skinheads/ex skinheads will state they wouldn't change a thing. Not so in my case, for as I have said the nights of getting out of my face on alcohol would most certainly change. I can go to a ska event today and dance myself stupid on J20s listening to sounds that spread love and happiness, with not a fear in the world of having a bottle cracked over my head. I am 58 on my next birthday, way too old to chance. As the saying goes, "I'll die with my boots on".

PAUL WILLO

I have to be honest and say that the thing that got me into skinhead was a combination of music and style. The menacing look was great, I thought. It came to me with the 2 Tone boom and it's stuck with me ever since. It's an attitude as well Skinhead - don't suffer fools, have pride in yourself, work hard, play hard. Skinhead when I was young was about camaraderie and still is, to an extent. Bank holidays to the coast in the hot sun at Scarborough, clashing with Teddy boys and Mods. We had a great time. Going to charity shops trying to find good 60s suits was another thing we used to enjoy doing. Hanging around on corners with tape decks playing - we even played them with the batteries running out, lol. Violence was a big factor as well. We were council estate kids with tough upbringings - you had to be able to look after yourself.

The music was brilliant. 2 Tone led us back to the original ska n reggae, then we also liked punk and some Oi!, exciting times growing up. People crossing the road from you when they saw you coming, lol - was very funny but felt good at the same time, lol - We certainly pulled the ladies! Think they liked the image more than anything else but we didn't care, lol.

The gang element was a great crack: we had good friends through it and lost some good friends on the way. Gigs, trips out, Once 2 Tone fell away we held our own music nights as the right wing had gained a bit of momentum in the scene and being a skinhead meant you were automatically racist and on one day, a Saturday I recall, I was attacked in Leeds city centre by a gang of black youths and given a right pasting simply cos of how I dressed. A big black bloke saved my skin and dragged me away by my legs LOL. I got home that same day to York, went out and then was beaten up by a black guy in York, a good day but it was part and parcel of the skinhead thing - you had to take the rough with the smooth but I didn't hold it against them. Skinhead and the racism matter will always be about; it'll never die, especially in the media and those who aren't clued up. Does it spoil the scene? Yes it does, but that's life unfortunately, and you have to make a stand when necessary.

The years passed by and we saw the late 80s boom and I started promoting, Desmond Dekker I put on--what a night and occasion that was. I created the Street Feeling ska fanzine, which was very popular at the time and went all over the world. I love the ska scene, especially through the 90s, it was a great close knit community of diehards. The reformation of bands in the 00s saw more people back in the scene but the close knit feel has been flooded, although those of us who were friends through the 80s n 90s still are friends, which is great.

My love musically is The Specials. I wrote 2 books on the band and got to work with them on tour, which was the thrill of a lifetime. I was at Bestival onstage with them for that first-ever gig in 2008 when they were billed as the secret act. I still promote gigs, have done now for over 25 years as YorkSka Promotions and I run the Specialized project, a ska music-based charitable project that raises money for teenage cancer trust, youth music UK and smaller charity groups. Mixing great community spirit with great music makes one hell of a powerful force. Skinheads are there supporting as well, which is superb, it's the best subculture out there, always has been, always will be... Paul Willo -Specialized Project October 2015

JOHN RICHARDS

Some early skinhead memories: well, there was a gang of us: Tonka, AJ, Spotty, Splott, Mark G, oh the memory has dimmed a bit, but there was one guy I had a run in with (it was very tribal at the time, before all the football crap started). Now he was a big guy! Anyway, something kicked off and he started mouthing at me, so I slugged him. He didn't even move backwards! 'Outside' he said, so out I went and he stood in the doorway (he filled it!) and he shouted, 'Come back in at least you had the balls to come out'. Was I pleased or what. His name was Vud!

There was only 3 of us from my village and then there was a gang from Bridgend: Ollie, Jasper and a few others, well they started on us one night, Ollie ended up going through a window, and most of the others went over a wall and onto a dried-up riverbed (it was mid-summer). Sgt Basil Craddock came along and everything stopped! "What's going on here then?" Ollie was getting out of the window, there was us 3 standing (cuts and bruises all over) and Craddock heard the moans coming from over the wall, he looked over and there was this mass of writhing bodies. He looked at us, grinned, and said, "Cefn's that way." He was a right hard ole bastard, if he clipped you, you weren't booked. So he let us off, then he found out we'd already sorted the bouncers and owner out and were banned from the Palais De Dance for life. Summer 1971, ole Craddock had caught up with us and made us pay for the window, he was genuinely pleased that we'd stood our ground and came out on top that night.

So Me, Des and Chris became celebs that night! But my real claim to was the night there was a ruckus in the Kee Klub, Tyrannosaurus Rex were there, and Bolan started dissing us from the small stage (he was an utter big headed, big mouthed twat then!) He was half giving it the big I am, fucking Skinheads, what are you troublemaking thick fucking cunts doing in here, you fucking Neanderthals! So I jumped up on the stage and nutted the fucker out. The place was in uproar. They never reopened the place after we left. (The reason you can't mention it is the owners are still alive and still pissed at what happened). Oh, I was a little bastard when I was young. But we all were in some way or another. I fuckin' hate T Rex!

Another memory I've got is from the summer of 71. I had a new bit of arm candy, met her down town to go for a quiet drink (Sun evening) had my White Levi Stay- Prest on, Brogues and Sherman, walked in the back room (music room) of the 3 Horse Shoes, she was right behind me, Oh my days. It was FULL of bikers. (If I'd been own my own I would be on my toes). In I go, all you could hear was Sssskinhead and spitting! Got my pint and her cider, sat down and they were all giving it the big one. Paranoid and Black Night on the jukebox. So I go up and put Slade on 'Get Down and Get With it'. Anyways, I had to go have a piss (the men's was a zinc sheet construction at the end of the courtyard). I had my piss and I could hear Clomp, Clomp, biker boots. I thought 'here we go'! He stuck his head round the corner and 'cracked' I gave him a fucker, over he goes! Then they all came running. I told them 'one at a time not all together'! The guy I'd smacked came too and said, "I only came out for a fuckin Piss!" Oops.

Everything calmed down and I was accepted into their company! Had a brilliant night with them! And for a while, after I walk in a pub where they were, I'd get my pint and go sit with them, mortal enemies drinking together, we didn't half get some looks, I had a few rucks with some others who would come and join them (bikers). There was one who wanted a go, but never gad the bottle to shout out. Big Terry who was the de-facto leader of them told this guy one night that if it kicked off between me and the guy, Terry would put his last £5 on me to win!! Well, all aggression drained from him!

JOHN ASHMAN

 I was first a skinhead back in 82 at the age of 15. I was searching for something as I had had a bad childhood at home and was at a children's home. I was very lost and disillusioned with life. In the children's home was a skin who I connected with. I loved their style and we had a mutual connection through our upbringing and bad experiences. Through playing the old 45s on the communal record player I started to hear some Ska and 2 Tone. I instantly loved the music. I couldn't wait to get my first DM's and get into the style of clothes. There were maybe 15 skinheads in the town of Frome at that time and they in a way became my family during that time. I made a lot of mistakes as a lad growing up, but being part of that since back then probably saved my life.

I did leave the scene for a long time after but have been back on the scene again in recent years and love it. Again, it's the style, the music, the people that make it what it is. I'm glad that the scene is returning in a big way with gigs, weekends, rallies happening all the time. Being a skin has again given me an identity and a belonging and I would not change it.

JOHN HAWKER

Well it was in the summer of 1965, I was a sixteen year old Mod. I had a Vespa GS160. I lived in a small town called Portishead, about 10 miles from Bristol city centre.
Portishead was a quiet place, with a sea front and what was called the lake grounds, i.e. boating lake and play areas for families to enjoy themselves.

Not much for us to do, except local discos. On Sunday afternoons we would all meet down at the lake grounds to listen to the latest sounds on numerous radios, it was a normal afternoon, music blaring out. But the sounds were soon quite loud: the rockers (or grebos as we called them) had rode their greasy bikes to the lake grounds, the noise was deafening. You could see a mile off they wanted trouble. They out-numbered us two or three to one, as normal. Most of the so-called mods ran off, and left a few of us to get on with it, they knew I would not run. Well it started, I remember getting some punches and kicks in and then nothing. I woke up, looked around and saw nobody, except the local cops and ambulance, I was hurt bad: my jaw broken, my nose broken, my right fist was fucked, and my right arm broken. I was in a bad way. In fact, I had been beat to fuck. My ribs were hurting like hell; I was in a lot of pain.

Well that was the lesson I needed, fuck the local MODS. When I had recovered from the beating, I went up the town (Bristol) on my scoot, I went to find the Never on a Sunday boys, after hearing a lot about the so-called crew, and they had a hell of a reputation.

It seemed a safer bet, well, I found the Never on a Sunday café. On going in after parking scoot outside with the rest of scoots, went in and nobody took any notice that I was a new face in there, I got the nod off a few lads-not knowing then that we would become good friends. It was or it seemed just like any other café, but something was different. I could not work it out, was it the music from the juke box was it that the--- well I never worked it out, the music was reggae, good reggae.

Well, after chatting to a lot of the lads there, I felt safe being there. After that I went there a few times, I had to find out who the top man was. Then one evening a bloke bigger than me walked in, it was the man called Willy Pasco, top man with his brother Angelo. It was Angelo that kept us all together, after a few weeks I got accepted as one of the never boys. There was a lot of things going on.

The best time was when we fought the Bristol chapter of Hells' Angels. It started on a Tuesday night, when one of our skin girls got hit with a chain outside the Locarno. I was with about a dozen lads drinking just up the road, the word came to us, so we ran like hell and found the angels still there-- need I say anymore? We battered the fuck out of them, a few got stabbed. We done, but that was just the start.

The next night they were in town again, more fighting. Fights were breaking out all over Bristol: it went on until one of the angels got run in to a wall on his bike. He died later. The police were everywhere: our café, our local pubs, but they never found out anything. Well, on the following Saturday the police wanted us to call a truce with the angels, so after a big meet called by Willy, we all agreed to settle it. So we agreed to the meet, it was held on college green a large area at the bottom of park street, Willy shook hands with Maverick Hell's Angel leader with everybody cheering. The police thought it was all over. Was it hell.

Apart from a bit of Paki-bashing no, we were never racist. How could we be? Our music came from Jamaica and a lot of our crew were Jamaicans, so they had no rights to call us racist.

Although I'm still a skinhead, I'm not into the scene anymore. I'm too old now –66. I left the Never as an active skin in 1972 after six years. All I can say is I've had a good life living as a skin. I still wear Dr. Martens, Levis, Bracers, Ben Sherman shirts, Sta-Prest when I go out to town; yes I still get up there. Over the years with the Never I became the top man.

The Never on Sunday boys still exist, about 50 of us and we do a lot of charity work, it's a way of putting something back to society what we took out years ago.

We were frowned on by many because of the way we dressed. They called us thugs, but I didn't care, I was happy being a skinhead and I'm still happy.

Bank Holidays were the most violent, mainly at sea side resorts i.e. Bournemouth-Weymouth- Torquay- anywhere. The best were at Weston Super Mare Monday Bank Holiday. There always were bikers down there and loads of different crews from all over the place many, many, running battles with bikers and police-- real good fighting—brilliant!!

JASON GODDARD

 My name is Jason Goddard and I was born in Sheffield in 1972, where I had a very typical 1970's upbringing. Roundabout 1980-82 I first noticed a good friend of mine at school had started to come to school with his hair shaved short, dressed in boots, tight jeans with turn ups and check shirts. To my knowledge, his parents were Skins and naturally they wanted their little boy to be a Skin too. I looked up to this friend of mine and was really impressed with the way he looked, it was very different from the flares, platform shoes and long hair that I had seen on a daily basis throughout the 1970s... Ya know-- the stereotypical Council Estate hippy/glam rock kind of look.

Around this time I had also become very aware of a new kind of music, a type of music that was sang by a bald-headed fella called Buster Blood Vessel who wore jeans, braces and boots on stage and in his videos, along with other bands such as Madness and The Specials. They all had songs that had a fundamentally reggae type beat, which of course I didn't recognise at the time, but they all had a certain crazy energy and stage presence on Top of The Pops, which of course I did recognise and I loved it... all I knew was that I was hooked.

Not long after this, I was taken to a local shoe shop by my Grandma, with strict instructions from my Mum that I was to buy a new pair of "sensible school shoes, to go back to school in at the end of the 6 weeks holidays". Once I got to the shop that was very well-known in our area, I then proceeded to convince my Grandma that the reddish brown coloured boots in the shop window looked the most hard wearing and smartest, and therefore would be the most suitable for everyday at school...

They were of course a pair of Oxblood Doc Martens, my first-ever pair and I was made up with them, I even enjoyed polishing them and I still do today, for hours on end in fact, much to my wife's amusement.

Doc Martens are iconic and as much a part of the scene as anything else. Once I got my new pair of Doc Martens I was then met with a very familiar question, that was put to me on the upstairs deck backseats of the bus, (as that's where all the Top Boys sat)... "So what colour laces tha gunna ave in em then?" "Eh? Wot thy on abart?" I asked, completely puzzled. It turned out that there were lots of rules based around the different meanings associated with different coloured laces, white being white power, red meaning you had given someone a good kicking etc. Wow, how could it all be so complicated? But I didn't care, I was loving every minute of it and I soon realised that the rules varied from town to town and region to region and they were all a load of complete bollocks at the end of the day.

Once I had my Dockers, as we call them round my way, I then needed the rest of my "Skin uniform" and I soon talked my mum into buying me some "new school trousers" called Sta-Prest from a well-known shop in the Sheffield markets called Harrington's, no connection to the jacket of the same name, but ironical as it is where I also got my first Harrington jacket from as well. The Fred Perry T-shirt and green "bomber jacket" soon followed.

My Mum was horrified at my new look and interest in the style, as the papers soon became full of stories about "Bovver boys" in their "Bovver Boots" and the pitch invasions at our local Sheffield Wednesday football ground by Skinhead thugs, looking for a fight. The schools soon banned the "crew cut" hair style, along with our Dockers as a result of this, so I ended up in black DM shoes with my school uniform instead, as two fingers up to their authority.

I naturally drifted out of the scene as a kid, because the clothing I wore was still paid for by my parents and they refused to buy me more "Bovver Boy" stuff, but I still listened to Ska and 2 Tone and it was always in my heart.

Once I had grown to be 18 and moved out into my own place, a shit hole flat on the 10th floor of a block of flats, in a well-known shitty area in Sheffield, I naturally started drifting back in to the Skin scene as, like I say, it was still in my heart. I bought Ska compilation cassettes and as much Madness, Bad Manners and Specials stuff as I could get my hands on. I was completely skint as there wasn't much work around at the time and I took to making my own "Homebrew" beers and lagers so that I could afford to drown my sorrows of being stuck in that shitty flat with no money, hardly any friends and equally few prospects.

I soon got chatting to a kid called Mark who we shared a mutual friend with and it soon became evident that we had a lot in common, particularly when it came to Boxing/Martial Arts, Music, films and a general way of life. We would spend hours and hours playing darts in the hallway of my shitty little flat, listening to Ska and getting pissed on the homebrew that I had made with loads of extra sugar in it, so as to make it even stronger... It tasted like stale piss but a 2 litre pop bottle full of that stuff could tranquillise a baby rhino and was the cause of many a dart hole in my ceiling and surrounding walks and doors... I think I even have a few scars on my feet and legs as a result of pissing around on that home brew.

Anyway, I had a video cassette of "Beneath the Skin" taped off the TV and narrated by my now Facebook friend Symond Lawes, who runs the Skinhead Reunion, whilst being very active in the scene and me and my pal watched it over and over, getting more and more determined to get back into being a Skin. This was harder for my pal Mark than it was for me, as at the time he had a ponytail as a tribute to one of his favourite actors Steven Segal, but I soon put that right during a heavy home brew drinking session, when I dug out my hair clippers and his ponytail was soon in his lap, no longer attached.

I then set about "obtaining" as many Richard Alan books as I could from WH Smiths, along with a first edition of "The Skinhead Bible" that I still have today. I set about buying some new Dockers with some Christmas money that I had saved up and I managed to get a great Donkey jacket from an old girlfriend's dad and I decided I was going to be a Skin again.

However, I soon found that the scene had changed quite dramatically from what I naively remembered as a child. Due to my age, politics had never been a factor for me and neither had racism, as I only knew a couple of mixed race people in my town and they were sound with me so why should I dislike them? Now, as I said earlier, I was born in 1972 when PC did not exist, the TV, radio and even kids' cartoons had racist, sexist and religious content and I don't just mean now and again, I mean pretty much all day, every day.

Naturally people grew up believing that certain names for foreigners were acceptable and why shouldn't they? They didn't know any better and most people had never seen, let alone gotten to know an immigrant, so they had no idea how offensive and hurtful certain terms and names could be. This doesn't make it ok, it simply makes it a fact.

People around the country's capital and living in and around ports and coastal towns got to meet and work and even live in a more multicultural community than most people, so they naturally gained an education and respect for multiculturalism. Sadly, the surrounding areas took a fair bit longer to gain this education and racism was unfortunately a way of life for the majority of British people, as it is for most indigenous people in other countries that are experiencing immigration and multiculturalism for the first time.

They/we knew no better and it is a completely human response to fear the unknown and then as a coping mechanism to attack or simply poke fun at what scares you the most, in an attempt to show strength. This isn't an excuse and it doesn't make this type of behaviour acceptable, but I don't care where you are from, what colour you are or what your religion is etc., you have acted in this way in the past at some point and you will act this way again if you are scared or confused, simply because it is a human response... Nothing to do with race, colour or culture etc.

Now as I started to say, I noticed a big change in the 8 or so years that I had been away from the scene and now there was much criticism of immigrants and immigration, mainly due to a shortage of jobs and money. God knows I experienced this shortage myself for long enough and there seemed to have been a massive change in the scene.

In my mind, the change in the scene came along with the country's general attitude of bitterness and anger towards anyone who might possibly take away our jobs, our housing and our benefits and, God forbid, our women.

This was also reflected in the far more aggressive style of music that was now being played by bands such as Skrewdriver and other Oi bands, to accompany the racially inflammatory remarks that were being made loudly in the pubs and in the streets. This anger also presented itself in general violent acts, along with racially motivated acts of violence, all out of ignorance and frustration at our

Government. Not to mention the increase in swastika tattoos, Union Jack T-Shirts and BNP, National Front and Combat 18 graffiti that sprung up all over the place.

Through a period of time like this, I can honestly say that I never got caught up in acts of violence related to politics, race or even football, but the opportunities were certainly there. I have always been a fighter, in and out of the ring from 9 years old. I have a strong sense of right and wrong and have been a little outspoken over the years when it comes to things that are important to me, like family and loved ones etc. and this has landed me on the wrong side of the law on many occasions, but I have never fought over politics, race, religion or football.

The scene all felt very angry and political to me now which I wasn't very comfortable with at all and I immediately noticed that I would get a lot of derisory looks in the streets and on the bus, not to mention getting followed by security guards in every shop I ever went in. I soon realised that it wasn't for me after the changes that the scene had gone through, I wasn't making a statement, I wasn't racist, well at least no more racist than anyone else who grew up in my town in the same era.

I soon realised that being a Skin in this new era wasn't going to be conducive to finding work or settling down with a girl' n having kids, while ever I was going to be tarred with the same brush as the White Power Skins from America that were getting so much press coverage. In my mind, those are the people who ruined the true Skinhead scene and who still taint its image even to this day, and will do for many years to come.

Inevitably I drifted away from the scene again but I still always wore the Harringtons, albeit with a Ralph Lauren badge on it, Ben Shermans, the Fred Perrys and Dockers, but I did it in a much more toned-down manner so as to be more accepted in social situations. I did keep the crew cut and razored in parting though for over 25 years.

No doubt some small-minded people will criticise me for this behaviour in much the same way that they will criticise me now because I have come back into the scene after 20 years, as a "re-born", as some would call me. And you know what? I don't give a fuck! I am me and I do what makes me happy and if my family and I are all good, then fuck the rest...take me or leave me as you find me.

It is essential to move with the times whilst keeping tradition and a passion in your heart for what you love the most and that is exactly what I have done. In the last few years that I have come back to the Skin scene, I was an extra in 'This Is England', which I love. I have met more of my childhood heroes and musicians than ever, I have been to more live gigs than ever, bought my first fully custom scooter and been to more scooter rallies than ever before, been to more Ska and Reggae music festivals than ever and have made more friends than ever and you know what? I fucking love it!

It seems to me that it is going back to how it was and should be, with The Spirit of 69 in everyone's heart. The World has changed and will continue to change and now I know with the benefit of some maturity and hindsight, that life is all about education, understanding, acceptance, respect and forgiveness. Live life to the full by treating people how you would like to be treated yourself, have good manners, good morals and be polite and courteous. Give up your seat for someone more in need of it than you, hold a door open for someone and smile at a complete stranger. Then hopefully, just hopefully, good things will happen to good people...and if they don't, then at least you have the satisfaction of going to your grave knowing that you did your best to be a good person and to get along with others to the best of your ability, but make sure you live your life doing what makes you happy and not at the expense of others.

Skinhead is a beautiful but often brutal sub-cult, founded in a time of very little tolerance and based around rejection of authority and a hatred of anything and anyone other than the brotherhood of Skin. Having said that, different mobs of Skins in the same town would still fight against each other and when a Ska or Oi gig was on in my home town of Sheffield, the local Skins would converge on the train station waiting for Skins from other cities who were coming to the gigs and then battle would commence.

Times have of course changed, some people have changed completely and others just partly, but some not at all. In short, Skins get shit from other Skins and they always have done due to its system of hierarchy like a pack of wild wolves, but they also have an inbuilt camaraderie that you won't find anywhere else-- other than in the military. This is why so many ex-military personnel become Skins. Brutal maybe, but a gang of Skins was also a beautiful thing, as it was also a surrogate family for those who had no family of their own or even worse, had a family that only offered pain and abuse to its members.

The brotherhood of Skin is many different things to many different people but ultimately, in a military fashion, it will break you down initially, to weed out the wheat from the chaff, then rebuild you back up, and then embrace you as one of its own. Sadly, some people enjoy the breaking down of others part of the system just a little too much and do it just for the sake of their own perverse needs, quite often out of frustration, pain and a hatred of themselves.

Some have been Skins and now have nothing left and their childhood hatred has festered, but most people with this vindictive and out-dated mentality never were and never would be accepted by true Skins, so they have no other option but to pretend and to search out confrontation and launch an attack, but only ever on a cyber-level, as they could never survive in the real world and amongst the real brotherhood of Skin.

Wear your uniform with great pride, polish your boots, play your Skinhead reggae loud, skank as often as you can and most of all... Be happy.... Be a Skin!

DEAN COUGHBOROUGH

 I think I became a skinhead through a combination of things. I was a very shy, ginger kid with braces on my teeth and glasses when I started senior school in 79, the same year Madness, the Specials and Selecter were on Top of the Pops. The whole 2 Tone look swept the playground almost overnight and I just fell in love with it all, I suppose , Sta-Prest, white socks and brogues, Harrington, etc. and DM's when I'd saved enough for 'em.

Originally, me mum wouldn't let me cut me hair shorter than a no4, but I gradually sneaked it down to a no2 with a razor parting, when everyone else turned casual, after 2 Tone ended I just stuck with it. Nick Knights' book influenced my clothes and I got a lot smarter and 60s looking, leading to accusations of being a mod! Lol, skinhead from then on.

I'm not sure what it means to me now, l don't even know if I'd class myself as a skinhead because of my age, I've always been aware that it's a youth culture and I ain't a youth. It shaped me when I was a kid and gave me confidence and a sense of belonging to which I'll always be grateful - now I just consider myself to be a well-dressed middle aged man with short hair and a lot of records.

I have a lot of memories, not all good, but standout one would be the Isle of Wight scooter rally 85: my first run, pissed down with rain and 6 of us sharing a two man tent, Bad Manners and Desmond Dekker live on stage, warm beer and dodgy bogs, but over 20,000 people there and an adventure out of South London.

Violence was really an everyday occurrence - from playground to streets eventually to pubs and clubs. Despite coming from a boxing family, I was never a natural fighter and usually got more hidings than I gave out, the main thing was not to run. I've got scars on my fingers from getting glassed in the Gun Tavern in Croydon and one on my head from a pool cue, there were some major tear ups back then against casuals and black kids and you stuck together, win or fuckin' lose. That was probably the same for every teenage boy in every city and town around the country, though. Some scary times, especially when Stanley knives became popular.

It's funny looking back at the scene then regarding politics, we just seemed to rub along together, there was always a national front element and it was never for me as I have black relatives, but racist attitudes were common place in those days and I just ignored it, until I'd say around 85/86 when the RAC/ Blood and Honour stuff became prevalent and we became seriously divided. By then I started going to northern soul do's and blues parties and toned down the whole look to a more suedehead look. I've always believed in workers' rights and was often called a commie and because of my love for reggae got called a nigger lover regularly, that was really the end of me associating with other skinheads, apart from a few sussed northern boys I knew from the scooter rallies.

Favourite artists in the strictly skinhead sense, I'd have to say Prince Buster, I met him in 2000 and he bought me a beer and had a proper chat with him, his fabulous Greatest Hits was one of the first records I ever bought. I was a bit different in the fact that I bought the current reggae music at the time, as well as the boss stuff, so I had (still have) Dennis Brown, Gregory Isaacs, Yellowman, etc. from the 80s. As for clothes -my first tonic suit, tan and blue, with a beige/blue /yellow stripe oxford weave Ben Sherman, ox blood brogues and my black Crombie. I went down the pub dressed in that when I was 17 and the reaction from the old villains and gangsters that drank in there was something else, most had been original skins and their approval meant EVERYTHING to me at that age.

GARY WITTS

 Went to 3 different senior schools, left school with no qualifications. Me and my mates became skins in the late seventies, we grew up on one of the largest council estates in Europe, Chelmsley Wood. It was quite a violent place in them days: you were either a skin, punk, mod, or a nobody. There was quite a group of us, had clashes with other groups on the wood, it was separated into areas, in them days we were from area 13. Another neighbouring estate was Shard End, we always had scuffles with them (they were skins)-beat me up quite bad one time. We paid them back. But sometime later we became great friends with that same group- still friends with some of them till this day.

We would have done anything for each other and did at times, we got up to all sorts, had some great times. None of us have done too bad in life, some no longer with us, RIP. I have always been a grafter. I had 7 kids: 5 sons, 2 daughters, none have become skins, yet some of the older ones love listening to the stories of when we were skins, don't tell the x rated ones.

One of my best mates on the photo I sent you became 6-time Mr Olympia, lives in Marbella now. Great times being a skinhead, our group were like a family. I really felt like I belonged. Whenever any of us meet we talk about those days. I have had a great life since then, ups and downs, but I always love thinking back to them days. They were special times never to be forgotten.

MARTIN LONG

 It all started in late '79, when 2 Tone appeared in the record shops, on my radio (no pun intended) etc., it was so much better than the cheesy tunes that was around for the young-sters to listen to. There was this new wave punk era that exploded a few years earlier, but not everyone wanted to have a Mohican, zips and safety pins holding their clothes together, so for the inner city kids, the ska revival was much needed and gladly taken under the wings.

This is when the new skinheads were being introduced to the "original Skinhead or Hard Mod" music and clothes, listening to the blue beat and Jamaican R'n'B, which the early Mods listened to which was later given the name of "SKA", through to the smooth soulful Rocksteady and onto the Boss Reggae Sounds of Trojan, Pama and their subsidiaries and lesser known labels like Crystal, Ackee, Bamboo, Blue Cat, Pyramid, Sioux and so on.

In late '82, some of us went into the Scooter Scene riding Lambretta's and Vespa's, and in the Scooter Scene, there was 2 types of rallies, one for the Mods in their Parka's and Boating Blazers at places like Brighton, Southend and Isle of Wight and another set of rallies at different locations or seaside resorts around the UK like Morecambe, Great

Yarmouth, Weston-Super-Mare and Exmouth, run by Chris Burton of Torch Promotions who was also the resident DJ at the Northern Soul club The Torch in Stoke.

On these rallies you would see Scooter Skins, Scooter Punks, Scooter Psychobillies and Scooterists who would wear anything from Army Greens, MA1 Flight Jackets, Jean Jackets, DM's and so on, no suits, as camping in a muddy field with nowhere to keep your clothes dry and not creased.

I got into being a DJ purely as a laugh at first, a landlord of a local pub in Portsmouth asked me and a mate if we knew anyone who could DJ as his regular DJ had let him down, so we went and got our record players, small speakers and boxes of records, and after that it just took off. Hired the proper kit and I started doing scooter clubs events as main DJ, birthday parties for my mates, pub do's etc. I enjoy hunting for those forgotten or unknown tunes as I absolutely love the buzz of playing for the crowd, and seeing everyone getting up and filling the floor.

When I was asked to DJ at the 40th Anniversary of the Skinhead movement at Margate, I could not decline such an offer, to be part of something so big and to spins some tunes too. What was even better was Jennie Matthias was the first act on and didn't have a sound man, and I was asked if I would do it, it was a pleasure and an honour to do it, and afterwards was invited on stage with her as she performed her recent releases. Then came the 40th Anniversary of the Skinhead Movement being held in Cardiff to remember the events in nearby Weston-Super-Mare and Swansea and again asked to be one of the DJ's playing a selection of Traditional Ska, Rocksteady and Reggae.

It has been good to see Skinheads from all around the world at various events such as Margate, Brighton, Cardiff and with no aggro, no politics, no football rivalry, whereas in the late sixties and the ska revival, skinhead supporters from visiting football teams would be "having it on their toes" with each other. But everyone is so much more relaxed now, no rivalry, no turf wars as they would call it, everyone is there for one reason: "the way of life" as a skinhead, the music, the clothes, and the sense of humour.

As for the clothes, from Ben Sherman, Fred Perry, Lambretta, Relco button-down "window pane" check shirts, or a plain white button-down shirt, Fred Perry polo shirts, Sta-Prest, Dogtooth or Prince of Wales check trousers, Levi 501's & Lee jeans, with red, white, blue, green and even yellow socks with DM's, Loafers, Brogues, Dealer Boots, Crombies with the red hankies, Sheepskin coats, Tonic Suits with the 3 or 4 peak hankie to match with the colour of the shirt being worn, the skinhead takes pride in his appearance.

The media's misinterpretation of skinheads as being racists thugs, considering tradition or original skinheads have a love and excellent knowledge of black music no matter if it is Ska, Rocksteady, Reggae, Soul, Motown, or 60's R'n'B, and are often seen at Northern Soul and Reggae events and as collectors or DJ's or record dealers and a person for the enjoyment of black American or Jamaican music.

ACKNOWLEDGEMENTS

Today the skinhead scene is alive and kicking more than ever. Skinhead events are organised regularly, which sees a mixture of both traditionalist revivalist skins, as well as a whole new generation of skinheads all come together. Annual events are held at the likes of Margate and Brighton, which sees skinheads from all over the world in attendance.

This book wouldn't have been possible had it not been for the help and support of many to whom I'm eternally grateful. Firstly, I'd like to thank my best mate on the skinhead scene, Dave Ealand, for putting me in touch with his many contacts for the purposes of interviewing. Not only that, but must note here, Dave Ealand is also the guy who came up with the great book title – Skins: Oxblood, Sweat & Beers. Cheers for that matey and this book may not have been possible had it not been your help. Love you, mate!

It was a great honour to have two members of The Specials on board – Neville Staple and Roddy Byers – and a big thank you to both of you as well as to Neville's lovely wife, Christine Sugary, who provided great help with this. And, of course, my mate Nick Welsh of reggae band King Hammond, and a true ska legend Mr Monty Neysmith. Thank you all guys, your efforts are very much appreciated.

In terms of research, I went through several press archives as I wanted to combine these with quotes from skinheads themselves to see how they contrasted. A number of television documentaries I was able to find, thanks to the internet, proved invaluable, as did the books *Skinheads* by Nick Knight and *Spirit of '69: A Skinhead Bible* by George Marshall and would like to thank both authors here.

I just want to thank all the guys that contributed their skinhead life stories here as it made for great reading, as well as supplying some of their photo collections: Kim Keanie,

Harry Brass, Bernard Nugent, Bob Weller, Steve Bawden, Ger'Snake Hughes, Henry Rutherford, Pete Griffin, Cai Roberts, Sheena Roberts, Ollie Roberts, Paul Molyneux, Chris Carrington, Sean Marshall, John Quelch, Jake Jones, Jason Hughes, Cat Lyons, Lizz Handley, Carl Woody Whitney, Steve Roworth, Frank Castle, Rob Eddols, James J Allen, Dave 'Toast' Rumsey, Barry Tracey, Paul Bond, Chris Richardson, Bill Newberry, Jim Lewis, Debbie Jones, Frank Struve, Wayne Smith, Ross Fergus Croft, Dave 'Boss' Griffin, Steve Campbell, Reverend Dave Ireland, David Webster, Paul Willo, John Richards, John Ashman, John Hawker, Jason Goddard, Dean Coughborough, Gary Witts and Martin Long: Thank you for all your time and efforts guys – all very much appreciated!

To all the team at New Haven Publishing for making this project possible, including Teddie Dahlin, and, finally, thank you all for all reading.

I hope this book has managed to educate some and has given you a taste of what being a real skinhead is all about, as it most certainly isn't racism or politics. It's about brotherhood, family, belonging, the music, the fashion – nothing more, nothing less. Keep the faith and long may the scene continue.

Ian Phillips
February 2016

About the Author

Born 9 September 1979, West Midlands, Ian Phillips had his first book published on Diana Ross in 2010. Prior to that he wrote a number of song-and-album reviews for a number of European-based websites. After attending King Charles I High School in his hometown of Kidderminster, he relocated to the North West of England and has worked in both theatre and television.

Ian released his hardcover and paperback coffee table size books titled Diana Ross Reflections in May 2015, and his ebook was made available in November 2015. Skins: Oxblood, Sweat and Beers is his third book.

Skins Oxblood, Sweat and Beers

Skins Oxblood, Sweat and Beers

Skins Oxblood, Sweat and Beers

Lightning Source UK Ltd.
Milton Keynes UK
UKOW06f2334230216

269003UK00014B/243/P